THE BEST THERE EVER WAS

DAN PATCH AND THE DAWN OF THE AMERICAN CENTURY

SHARON B. SMITH

Skyhorse Publishing

Skyhorse Publishing books may be purchased in bulk at special discounts for sales promotion, corporate gifts, fund-raising, or educational purposes. Special editions can also be created to specifications. For details, contact the Special Sales Department, Skyhorse Publishing, 307 West 36th Street, 11th Floor, New York, NY 10018 or info@skyhorsepublishing.com.

Skyhorse® and Skyhorse Publishing® are registered trademarks of Skyhorse Publishing, Inc.®, a Delaware corporation.

Visit our website at www.skyhorsepublishing.com.

10 9 8 7 6 5 4 3 2 1

Library of Congress Cataloging-in-Publication Data

Smith, Sharon B.
The best there ever was : Dan Patch and the dawn of the American century / Sharon B. Smith.
p. cm.
Includes bibliographical references.
ISBN 978-1-61608-585-8
1. Dan Patch (Race horse) 2. Harness racehorses--United States. I. Title.
SF343.D3S65 2012
636.1'75--dc23
2011042223

Printed in the United States of America

CONTENTS

PROLOGUE

WALT DISNEY LOVED Dan Patch. Or rather, he loved the idea of Dan Patch. He never saw Dan in person, but the great horse became a symbol of America to the Pied Piper of Americanism. When Disney was planning his first full-length live action film in the early 1940s, he chose to adapt a lovely little children's book, Sterling North's *Midnight and Jeremiah*. It was a perfect fit for Walt Disney: the story of an orphaned Indiana farm boy who saves an unwanted black lamb and wins a special prize at the county fair.

It took Disney more than five years to get the story into movie theatres. There were the wartime delays that bedeviled every studio, as well as financial problems growing out of several unsuccessful animated films and another partly live action film, *Song of the South*.

Mostly the problem was Walt Disney himself. He wanted the production of what he renamed *So Dear to My Heart* to be exactly right because it meant so much to him. It was to be his homage to small town America, born of a love he developed during four childhood years in rural Missouri.

Disney was determined to add his vision to Sterling North's, although the original book showed plenty of affection and admiration for rural life. To Walt Disney, turn-of-the-century America meant Dan Patch and he wanted the horse in his movie.

He had his screenwriters add an event that had never happened to him in Marceline, Missouri, although he certainly wished it had. The original book began with the birth of the black lamb, but Disney had the writers open with little Jeremiah Kincaid watching as Dan Patch's special railroad car stops in Fulton Corners, Indiana. The great racehorse is brought out to stretch his legs and have a shoe reset by Uncle Hiram, the local blacksmith. Disney picked a horse very much like the real Dan Patch to play the part, a dark brown beauty with a tiny white star. Jeremiah, like Walt Disney, was smitten and when the black lamb came into his life, he named it Danny.

Once Dan Patch was in the script, Sterling North himself rewrote *Midnight and Jeremiah* to add the Dan Patch scene. He then changed both Midnight's name and the title of the book.

So Dear to My Heart was released early in 1949 to good reviews but modest box office sales. Still, it remained one of Disney's favorites and figured in two of the most important steps later taken by his company. When he scheduled programming for his first weekly television series, *So Dear to My Heart* was placed near the top of the list of feature films to alternate with television specials. It was shown on the fifth episode of the series, on the day before Thanksgiving 1954, a slot that Disney figured would provide a huge family audience. Of all the feature films in the Disney vault, only *Alice in Wonderland* was broadcast sooner.

So Dear to My Heart also figured prominently in Disney's earliest concept of Disneyland. He hoped to build a miniaturized version of turn-of-the-century small town America, and Granny Kincaid's farmhouse was planned as a centerpiece. Disneyland eventually opened as a full-sized amusement park, but Disney clung to his idea in Main Street U.S.A., which still welcomes visitors to all the Disney theme parks. It represents Marceline, Missouri, where Disney lived from 1906 to 1910. Marceline was the model for Fulton Corners, Indiana, which welcomed Dan Patch in *So Dear to My Heart*.

What was it about Dan Patch that so captured the imagination of the man who gave the word "imagineer" to the lexicon? Part of it was the fact that the horse was so very good. As a child growing up in the Midwest, Disney would have heard about the unbeaten race record and the fastest harness mile in history. And part of it was the publicity. All the lithographs and posters and flip-card movies that promoted him must have appealed to the young artist who couldn't see the real Dan Patch but could see the next best thing.

But most of all it was because Dan Patch was so completely and utterly American. He rose up from next-to-nowhere to be the best there ever was in his sport, a uniquely American sport at that. He and his human partners lived what came to be known as the American Dream. The millions of people who loved him aspired to the dream themselves and some, like Walt Disney, wanted Dan Patch right there with them when their dreams came true.

1

DAN PATCH'S AMERICA

DAN PATCH REPRESENTED his time and place so perfectly that, if he hadn't existed, somebody might have tried to invent him. A few decades earlier, Horatio Alger's rags-to-riches Paul the Peddler and Ragged Dick embodied all the poor boys who succeeded in life by combining hard work and a trip out West, just as thousands of other Americans were doing.

A few years later, Edward Stratemeyer would make himself wealthy with stories of a youthful inventor whose discoveries mirrored early twentieth century American accomplishments. Stratemeyer created a pseudonym and a character: Tom Swift. Tom invented flying machines, space trains, and prototype televisions. Tom's Amazing Works (always capitalized and sometimes with an exclamation point) were what his young readers knew they might do, if only they were a little cleverer.

But unlike Ragged Dick and Tom Swift, Dan Patch was real. He didn't have to be invented and needed no fake name to tell his story, although his human handlers did take advantage of what the era had to offer to magnify what was already there. What was there was a turn-of-the-century everyman in the body of a very good racehorse.

Dan Patch lived, raced, and prospered at the very center of a changing America. In some ways, Dan's life at the center was literal. In the census of 1890, the geographical center of population had moved into Indiana. That's the point at which half the population lives to the east and half to the west, while half lives to the north and half to the south. By 1900, four years after Dan

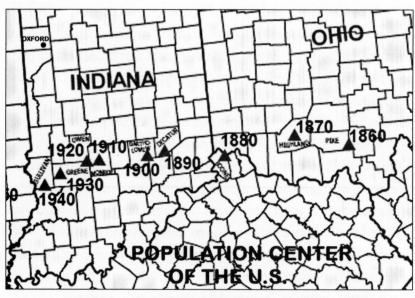

The population center of the United States remained in Indiana throughout Dan Patch's lifetime. *(Map: U.S. Census Bureau)*

was foaled, the point was into central Indiana, even closer to his birthplace in Oxford. In 1920, four years after his death, the center was well into western Indiana, continuing its westward journey into Illinois.

Although population doesn't necessarily mean wealth and importance, the center's movement across Dan Patch's home state coincided neatly with a shift in politics, money, and cultural significance, a movement that helped make a famous horse out of a good one.

Politics first: the almost exact division between Republicans and Democrats in Indiana and the other Midwestern states made the region a center of attention for politicians. Indiana alone had five citizens running for president or vice president in the twelve years preceding Dan Patch's birth. Three were Democrats. Two, including President Benjamin Harrison, were Republicans. Nobody knew which way Indiana would go, so the political power brokers of Washington and New York kept a close eye on news coming out of Dan Patch's state.

Then money: although the population center might still be moving west, the free frontier lands in the far west were gone by the time of Dan's birth. Farmland of the old frontier—the Midwestern states including Indiana—had become more valuable, even allowing for occasional recessions. Improvements in farm machinery, better railroads, and growing markets in the expanding cities made farming more lucrative for those who could afford to hold onto their acreage. There were fewer farmers than in mid-century, but the ones who survived had money to spend. They crowded the agricultural fairs, where harness racing was always the climax of the weeklong event.

Finally, culture: the writer of the late nineteenth century whose characters came closest to representing Americans as they liked to think of themselves was James Whitcomb Riley of Greenfield, Indiana, a small town much like Dan's hometown of Oxford. Riley wrote of "Little Orphan Annie" and the "old swimmin' hole" and driving a horse out to see "old Aunt Mary." He wrote of an idyllic time and safe, clean, prosperous places—mostly small towns.

James Whitcomb Riley of Indiana wrote of an idyllic small town America and the kind of people who came to revere Dan Patch. *(Photo: Indiana Teachers Association Booklet 1905)*

Most Americans of James Whitcomb Riley and Dan Patch's time didn't actually live in small towns, but rather on farms or in cities. But the towns represented the middle ground between the two, and people liked to imagine themselves there. So they loved Riley, who wrote of small town America, and they came to love Dan Patch, who represented the same thing.

When Riley wrote of a whistling boy "now unlocking in memory my store of heartiest joy" he tweaked the memories of both city people and farmers who never actually had the time to stroll about whistling when they were children, although they wished they had. Riley's death on July 22, 1916, was just two weeks after Dan Patch's own.

The Midwest, the former frontier, had reached the center of American life at the time of Dan Patch's birth, and midwesterners' opinions counted. In January of 1900, just as Dan reached racing age, the Republican Party chose Senator Albert Beveridge of Salisbury, Indiana, to articulate their position on international policy.

"God," announced Beveridge to the Senate on January 7, "has marked the American people as his chosen nation." It was a call to imperialism and, Beveridge said, control of the undeveloped countries of the world was "the divine mission of America." It looked like Dan Patch's small-town Midwest might be finding itself at the center of the world, not just the country.

As America moved to the middle in terms of numbers, so it did in terms of people. All the new factories and mills of the late nineteenth century meant a growth in middle managers and office workers, people who weren't rich but certainly weren't poor. They, and the comfortable farmers, had money to spend on enjoyment, but not so much that they could entertain themselves with summer houses in Newport or cruises to Europe. Instead, they took day trips to sporting events, fairs, and other public activities.

Equally important for Dan Patch and his fellow athletes, these new people of the middle had leisure time as well as extra money. Although most worked six days a week, they often had Saturday afternoons off. With money in their pockets, they were ready to head to the stadium or the racetrack. They could also afford to lay a small wager with bookmakers. Though usually illegal, bookmakers crowded every sporting venue.

During the thirty years before the birth of Dan Patch, American sports had begun their slow growth into their modern selves, with formal rules and operational structures. Some, like baseball, mostly originated in cities and large towns and greatly appealed to blue-collar people.

In 1871, the National Association of Base-Ball Players was organized. On May 4, the Fort Wayne, Indiana, Kekiongas hosted the Maryland Base Ball Club for what is considered the first-ever entirely professional baseball game. We don't know how many people showed up that day, but on May 5, people in Washington D.C. were amazed to hear that 3,000 paying customers crowded the field to see the Washington Olympics beat the Boston Red Stockings 10–1.

In 1876, a new National Baseball League brought the sport to even more cities. In 1882, the American Association arrived. The first World Series, which matched the Detroit Wolverines and the St. Louis Browns over fifteen games in the fall of 1887, attracted a total attendance of 51,000—an average of 3,500 per game. The organizers were pleased at the number of people willing to pay twenty-five cents to see a championship game.

Boxing appealed to many of the same people as baseball. The rough talking second generation Irishman John L. Sullivan became a true star in the 1880s, with small boys following him down the streets of Boston. In 1892, Sullivan faced a challenge by handsome young James Corbett.

"I can beat him without getting my hair mussed," Gentleman Jim boasted before the fight. He was nearly right, defeating Sullivan in a mere twenty-one rounds before 2,000 people, earning each boxer several thousand dollars.

On the other economic wing, football drew smaller crowds and earned little money for anybody, since it was primarily an amateur sport played at Eastern colleges. If baseball and boxing belonged to the lower classes, football was the property of the rich. It didn't bother football fans that only a few hundred people might watch an important game if the people who counted were there. The first stadium exclusively for football wasn't even built until 1903, and that was a modest affair at Harvard. An effort to create professional teams began about 1895, but the first league didn't appear until 1920.

Golf and tennis were around, but they existed for the players. Spectators, even at national championships, were mostly other players who wanted to see people play the game better than they could themselves. They were rarely charged admission and average people had never heard of the stars.

Looming above all these sports like a colossus was horse racing. Thoroughbred racing, where carefully bred running horses competed under saddle, and harness racing, where horses raced while pulling high wheeled carts or wagons, each drew huge crowds. Most tracks had a free field where working class people could attend. They couldn't see much, but they could bet. The tracks often had luxurious clubhouses where rich owners and their friends enjoyed excellent views. But, most of all, the tracks had grandstands and betting rings and concessions for the growing numbers of middle-income fans.

The National Base Ball League might proclaim itself satisfied with 3,500 people at a championship game, but as many people would come to see an ordinary race on an ordinary day. A crowd of 12,000 at a baseball game might rate a headline, but a few years before the Civil War, a race on Long Island drew

Goldsmith Maid drew 20,000 fans to a race in Saginaw, Michigan, in 1874, nearly half the population of the entire county. Harness racing was the country's most popular sport during the second half of the nineteenth century. *(Lithograph: Currier and Ives)*

somewhere between 70,000 and 100,000 people. Not surprisingly, nobody was able to count the crowd.

A top shortstop might wow people with his $3,500 a year salary, but a top trotter could earn more than that in one race. The trotting mare Goldsmith Maid averaged $28,000 a year in earnings over her thirteen-year racing career in the 1860s and 1870s, and a dozen or more lesser horses could expect to earn at least $10,000 a year.

The big names in harness racing were big names—period. When the famous driver Hiram Woodruff died in 1867 at the age of fifty, he was said to be second in renown only to General U. S. Grant. When Goldsmith Maid showed up at a race in Saginaw, Michigan, in July of 1874, she drew a crowd of 20,000. The last heat of the competition between the famous mare and her challenger, Judge Fullerton, was so thrilling that there was pandemonium in the crowded stands. One of the fans noticed a young woman depositing her baby on the ground in order to cheer the Maid to victory.

"Madam, your child!" the fan cried.

"Oh, I forgot all about Baby," the woman said. "But it makes no difference. I expect to have several babies, but I never expect to see another Goldsmith Maid."

The interchange was reported in a national newspaper, and it may or may not have been true. But what was true was the wide appeal of harness racing in nineteenth-century America. Men and women, young and old: everybody showed up at the racetrack.

At harness racing's peak in the late nineteenth century there were nearly a thousand harness tracks in North America. New "driving parks" were built across the country, including the West Coast, but harness racing became closely identified with the Midwest, thanks to important new tracks in Cleveland, Chicago, Saginaw, and other cities. Races held in conjunction with agricultural fairs also contributed to the importance of the sport to the Midwest, and vice versa. By the time of Dan Patch's birth in 1896, harness racing was truly the sport of the center.

It was not, strictly speaking, Standardbred racing as we know it today. There was an effort already underway to standardize pedigrees, but horses could still compete whether their bloodlines were "standard" or not. It was "light harness" racing and in most of the country drew more fans than Thoroughbred racing.

It was also a changing sport, but the changes merely created a more fertile field for the development of a star like Dan Patch. One alteration had occurred well before Dan came along.

There had been a brief flirtation earlier in the century with races between horses pulling vehicles as fast as they could, at a flat out gallop. But the Ben Hur-like free-for-alls were dangerous, with flipping carts and ejected drivers, and they proved almost impossible to bet on. The gallop was left to Thoroughbreds, and the middle gait between the walk and the gallop—the trot—was settled upon for harness racing. It was a good, consistent gait, one at which you could compare one horse to another, even if one raced in Ohio and the other in New Jersey. You could declare one horse best: the proof was right there in the stopwatch.

There was a period of several decades in which trotters competed under saddle, but by the second half of the nineteenth century, trotters competed under harness. Except that not all harness horses trotted.

Thanks to the melting pot origins of harness horses, for some of them the middle gait between the walk and the gallop was a pace, not a trot. In this gait, both legs on one side of the body move forward and back at the same time. In a trotter, the left front and right hind, for example, move forward while the right front and left hind move back—the standard locomotion technique for a four-legged mammal.

The pace earned no respect on the racetracks of the East. The fact that the pace was faster than the trot didn't matter. Possibly the wealthy people who helped support harness racing on the East Coast thought pacing didn't look quite right. Whatever the reason for the Easterners' bias, fans in the Midwest had no such prejudices.

Races for pacers, rarely scheduled on Eastern tracks, began appearing on Midwest fair programs shortly after the Civil War. Eventually, the fans couldn't be ignored and, by the 1890s, the pacing sport had its first true stars, horses who drew huge crowds wherever they appeared. Among them was Star Pointer, who was the first harness racehorse to reach the two-minute mile plateau. He did it in 1897, six years before a trotter managed the feat, pushed by two outstanding horses named Joe Patchen and John R. Gentry.

Another change in harness racing was less visible but equally important to the creation of the legend of Dan Patch. The horse as transportation was on his way out, and the horse as athlete was on his way in. It was not a sudden event.

The racing harness horse preceded the internal combustion engine by decades, and successful trotters were obviously athletes. But they weren't far removed from working horses.

Lady Suffolk, the best trotting horse of the first half of the nineteenth century, was discovered working as a carthorse on Long Island. Flora Temple, who came along ten years after Lady Suffolk, had her tail bobbed as a foal, since she was destined to be a working horse, a job she would have held if she hadn't been found to be so fast.

Flora Temple raced until 1861, the year before an Austrian engineer named Siegfried Marcus developed a little one-cylinder engine with a crude carburetor. Marcus had no particular use for his engine; he just wanted to see if he could make it run on distilled oil. But German engineer Gottlieb Daimler did have a use in mind. In 1886, he placed his more advanced, gasoline-burning version of the Marcus engine in front of a stagecoach and had himself a carriage that ran without a horse.

Harness racing fans in America knew nothing of the first use of an automobile. A few may have read about the second, but only the most perceptive of them would have thought it had anything to do with their favorite sport. Even when Massachusetts mechanics Charles and Frank Duryea built a horseless vehicle in 1893, most people probably thought the men were working on a hobby. Astute observers saw something else in the Duryeas' announcement in June of 1896, six weeks after Dan Patch was foaled in Indiana, that they had just sold their thirteenth vehicle. They got a glimpse of the future.

Even the less insightful knew something was up by 1901, when Ransome Eli Olds of Detroit announced that he was going to apply the concept of the assembly line to horseless carriages, because demand was too great to build them one by one. Automobiles clearly weren't going away.

They still seemed to a few people to be expensive toys, with only about 8,000 on the road in the U.S. when the Oldsmobile went into production. Those automobiles had to run on the same dirt and gravel roads that horses used, since hardly any American roadways had been paved with concrete. The vehicles got stuck, broke down, and otherwise became incapacitated at a far higher rate than horses did. By anybody's standards, horses were more efficient on the vast majority of roads.

Still, everybody was talking about automobiles. The number 8,000 represented an increase of almost 3,000 percent in six years. By the time Dan Patch had reached racing age, it was clear to almost everyone that end was in sight for the horse as a mode of transportation.

The fact that harness racing had begun its transformation into a pure sport rather than a representation of real life not only didn't hurt its popularity, it seemed to increase the excitement. Time, the quantification of speed, became everything. It wasn't just important that a horse won, but that he went fast. People would no longer have to pretend that that their carriage horses could go as fast as a Flora Temple, given good luck and expert training. The fast trotters and pacers were now recognized as uniquely talented, not just faster versions of ordinary horses. When it was clear they weren't ordinary, they could become stars that flamed as brightly as any celebrated human.

Late nineteenth century developments in communication made sure that news of racing accomplishments could be spread fast and wide. Innovations in printing had occurred in small steps since 1455, when Johannes Gutenberg amazed the monks

Joseph Pulitzer of the St. Louis Post-Dispatch and the New York World brought extensive sports coverage to American newspapers.
(Chromolithograph: Library of Congress)

of Mainz, Germany, with a bible produced from moveable type on a printing press.

Then in 1886 came Linotype, followed closely by the similar Monotype. These inventions mechanized typesetting, allowing an operator to sit at a keyboard, never actually touching type. Even a modestly skilled Linotype operator could set 350 lines an hour, rather than 350 words.

At the same time, both the telephone and the telegraph were becoming widely available in almost all parts of the United States. By 1900 there were 1.4 million telephones in the country, and some of the most enthusiastic users were newspaper reporters.

They had plenty of places to phone in their reports. In 1900 more than 2,000 daily newspapers were published in the United States; never before or since have there been so many. The growing American middle was responsible for the increased demand for newspapers, and part of the demand was for news of the sports that they were becoming so fond of. The *Spirit of the Times*, subtitled "A Journal of the Turf," had begun publication in New York in 1831, but its circulation remained modest for years. The new demand for sports coverage required something more.

It was provided by Joseph Pulitzer, a newspaper owner from St. Louis, whose understanding of the American heartland led him to add sports coverage to his publications. When Pulitzer acquired the *New York World* in 1883, a well-staffed sports department was one of his first and most important additions.

Pulitzer was known for his zeal for accuracy but also for his understanding of his audience. He was a man of the middle, and he knew what middle America wanted.

"Put it before them briefly so they will read it," he ordered his staff. "Put it clearly so they will appreciate it and picturesquely so they will remember it." Sports coverage seemed tailor-made for his guidelines.

Horse racing coverage was vital to the new sports sections of the *World* and its competitors, who now had to add sports to compete with Pulitzer. By the time Dan Patch reached the track, there was racing coverage in virtually every daily newspaper in the country, even partisan ones whose primary reason for being was to promote a cause or political party. Whenever a racing star appeared, every American could read about it.

The same influences of technology and demographics that led to sports coverage in American newspapers in the late nineteenth century helped create modern advertising. The growing middle class had discretionary money to spend, manufacturers had technological developments to help them produce massive quantities of their products, and newspapers were widely circulated to their best potential customers. Manufacturers turned in huge numbers to advertising. In mid-century, ads were simple affairs.

"We guarantee our celery malt compound," announced Dr. Barkley, whose mustachioed drawing was on each label. Ladies were urged to use "highly recommended almond nut cream." The portrait on the label didn't make it clear if the cream contributed to the elaborate hairdo shown on the model, or maybe to her flawless complexion.

With all the products to be sold and all the money to be had, it was inevitable that somebody would make it his goal to understand advertising. Among the someones was Albert D. Lasker of Chicago, another man of middle America.

"Give them a reason why," he said to manufacturers about their advertising. "Tell them what the product will do and why they should buy it."

By the time Dan Patch was making his name on the small tracks of Indiana a couple of years later, even a modestly successful horse feed manufacturer understood the concept. You could buy a good horse, make him a great one, and then tell the world that it happened because he ate your horse feed.

Finally, marketing was beginning to emerge. The use of a famous name to sell a product was found to be effective, as in the case of the Grover and Barber Family Sewing Machine vouched for by Mrs. U. S. Grant, who probably hadn't had to put her own hand to sewing for twenty years.

In the 1870s, the fledgling baseball leagues got their names before the public by having illustrated cards inserted in tobacco packages. These very early baseball cards didn't publicize individual players but rather the teams, and they proved unpopular. Baseball cards disappeared, then returned with a vengeance in 1909, after Dan Patch's phenomenally publicized racing career, with one star player illustrated on each card. Men and boys now collected the cards eagerly.

Clever promoters also discovered that it could be lucrative to publicize individuals simply to make them famous, knowing that the profits would be waiting further down the road. In 1876, John Burke created both the role of the modern press agent and the career of a western hero when he traveled from newspaper to newspaper talking up "Buffalo Bill" Cody. He offered them stories of Cody's exploits, exaggerated but not able to be discounted, and made him the talk of the country.

This was what was happening in America when Dan Patch was foaled in 1896. The middle class Midwesterner had become the quintessential American. He loved sports, had the time to attend, and the money to buy newspapers to read about them. What he loved most was horse racing, particularly harness racing, although baseball and football were trying to compete for his favors. Pacers particularly intrigued him, since they were faster than trotters.

Newspaper publishers, advertisers, and marketers had learned, maybe a little late and a little reluctantly, to understand the average American, and they now knew how to give him what he wanted. It turned out that he wanted a pacing star, and he was ready to embrace the one who came along as no horse ever had.

2

THE SHOPKEEPER OF
OXFORD, INDIANA

IT WAS LOVELY land for growing things, a fact recognized by the first human residents of the area. Those early people learned that you could actually stay put and still have enough to eat. Northwestern Indiana is the doorstep to the North American prairie, the glorious grassland that covered a third of the continent at the time Europeans arrived.

It was and remains a land of exceptionally rich soil, thanks to countless small creeks and streams that drain into the Wabash, then into the Ohio River. Snow melt from winter and plenty of rain through spring and summer have produced a thick black loam that will grow pretty much anything a person might want to plant.

What nature wanted to put down was grass. Where the prairie begins, near present-day Benton County and its former county seat of Oxford, the grass once grew so tall that man and horse could find themselves swallowed up by it. Early nineteenth century diary-keepers, men who joined parties looking for land to settle, vividly described what they saw. To one it was an "empire of bluestem," to another a "sea of grass." Nearly everybody talked about "grass as far as the eye can see."

A favorite Benton County story tells of a group of land-lookers who, in 1824, misplaced a member of their party when he foolishly rode his horse off the trail and into the grass. The others passed by without noticing, and the wayward settler suffered through several minutes of terror until he found his way back to his companions. He was lost in what we now call the tallgrass prairie, richer and more fertile than the shortgrass prairie further west. The tallgrass is largely gone today, thanks to its very richness, replaced by farmland.

The first residents of Benton County to figure out how to grow crops made scarcely a ripple in that sea of grass. They began their planting about the time Christ was born on the other side of the world, which makes them relative latecomers to agriculture. Ironically, the fertility of the land actually discouraged farming. The prairie was thick with well-fed buffalo and the woodlands just to the east were filled with smaller game.

With so much game, planting wasn't necessary, but it was useful. You didn't have to move camp so often if you had a dependable supply of food that stayed put. So the people learned to plant.

The settlers came to Indiana from the mountains of Virginia and Tennessee and Pennsylvania, from places where the land was hard and the soil was poor. Some came from England and

Ireland, where the soil might be good but the land was taken. They were farmers, most of them, and the rich black loam was not merely a happy bonus. It was their reason for moving and the land's reason for being.

The sea of grass became oceans of corn, wheat, and oats. But even as tallgrass was plowed under and fields replanted, farmers made a wonderful discovery. As good as the land was for growing

The limestone-rich soil of western Indiana proved ideal for crops and even better for raising livestock. *(Photo: Library of Congress)*

crops, it was just as good—possibly better—for growing live-stock. Bluegrass replaced bluestem.

Indiana farmers assumed that it was the black loam that made such high producing milk cows and strong healthy horses. But they were wrong, at least partly. The loam made the grass, but it was what lay under the loam that made the milk rich and the bones strong. Indiana sits on a foundation of limestone, and it's no coincidence that in all of the great horse breeding regions of the world, limestone lies under the soil. The Bluegrass Region of Kentucky, Newmarket in England, Normandy in France – each lies directly on a deep deposit of limestone. Calcium from the limestone finds its way into the grass and leaches into the water drunk by the farm animals.

The Messners followed the land west as the Indians moved out, but they weren't thinking particularly of farming, and not at all of horses. Michael Messner, son of German immigrants, was a carpenter, one of the best builders of barns in Western Pennsylvania. As a man watching for opportunity, Michael looked west. His wife, Catherine Clark, already had the call of the West in her blood, being Scotch-Irish.

In 1836, Michael, Catherine, and their three young sons left Cumberland County, Pennsylvania, for Ohio, where the forests were thick with oak and pine and where an ambitious carpenter could stock his business and clear himself a good sized farm at the same time. The other people moving west would need houses and barns on their new land. Daniel Messner Senior was eleven at the time of his family's move to Darke County, Ohio.

What people noticed most about Darke County was the timber. There were logs enough to build cities, if people came.

The logs were sufficient to cross Ohio with plank roads, if you could find the laborers to lay them. Messner prospered in New Madison, where he and Catherine settled. Michael built more barns and houses, amassing both money and land. When he was old enough, Daniel joined his father at his construction jobs, laying joists and pegging frames.

When he reached adulthood, Daniel Messner too heard of better land to the west. In Western Indiana, he was told, the soil was extraordinarily rich and farmers were clamoring for huge new barns for their flourishing herds of livestock. In January 1849, Daniel and his new wife Rebecca packed up and moved to Northwestern Indiana. Daniel bought 300 acres near Pine Village in Warren County and set about becoming an Indiana farmer.

He also continued his carpentry, and quickly became known for his timber-framed barns. Within twenty years, you would have been hard pressed to find a wood frame barn in the northern half of Warren County not built by Daniel Messner. As a farmer and barn-builder, Daniel appreciated horses and always kept several. They were working horses, not racehorses. Sport, he believed, was for men of leisure, and carpenters who also farmed had little of that.

As he approached fifty, Daniel retained his acreage, but began to drift away from both carpentry and farming. In 1874 he opened a dry goods store in Pine Village, the largest town in northern Warren County near his farm. He did well but recognized that he had to find a town with more prospects if he hoped to continue his climb up the economic ladder.

In 1877 he settled upon Oxford, a few miles to the north in Benton County. Oxford had lost its title as county seat, but it remained an important hub for farmers and travelers, thanks to depots for two major railroads. A merchant could make serious money in a town where farmers had to come to buy their goods and sell their crops. In November 1877, Daniel Messner closed his store in Pine Village and opened a new one in a handsome brick building on the public square in Oxford.

Daniel, his wife, and the youngest four of his nine children loaded their household goods into a four-horse wagon and traveled a muddy five miles from the farm to a house in Oxford. Among the children who made the move was Daniel's sixth son, sixteen-year-old Daniel Junior.

Young Dan was not a farmer, preferring to clerk in the store where his carefully chosen and stylish clothing would stay clean. Not that his health would permit the physically demanding life of a farmer. Even as a young boy, he suffered recurrent illnesses. Nothing serious, but enough to keep him out of the fields.

Daniel Messner Jr., Dan Patch's breeder and first owner shown in a 1905 postcard.

In his twenties, Dan noticed a little arthritis and began a lifetime of visits to mineral springs. But in spite of his health and his indoor job, he developed a deep and profound love of horses. His father didn't understand it, and young Dan didn't exactly understand it himself, but he was fascinated with horses.

But that was a sideline, a hobby. When his father's partner decided to sell his share of the Oxford store in 1885, twenty-four-year-old Dan became a full partner. At first he was primarily a clerk. He was gregarious and likeable and sold plenty of Panama hats to the men and finely stitched silk handkerchiefs to the women.

He became a specialist in choosing goods for the store, negotiating prices to ensure a profit, and displaying the items in a way that would attract the eye. He made buying trips by train to the big cities of the Midwest, particularly Chicago and Cincinnati, to select clothing and fabrics and sewing machines for Messner and Son to offer. He might spend $2,000 on a trip, a figure large enough to create a stir in Oxford and lure even more customers into the Messners' store.

Dan Junior settled into his career in merchandising just as traditional dry goods stores were transforming themselves into modern department stores in towns and cities across America. A frenzy of post-Civil War railroad building had ensured that almost every town big enough to support a store also had a depot, allowing distant customers to come into town.

Although Oxford never enjoyed a population much above 1,000, it was a commercial center, thanks to the two railroads and its location on a well-traveled road between Chicago and Indianapolis. The town might have been small, but nobody in Oxford considered it a backwater.

In 1892, Dan Messner married twenty-year-old Maud Marie Dodson, the daughter of a prosperous farmer from nearby Oak Grove. Maud's father, Elias, came from a prominent Virginia family, one with the misfortune to own land in Rappahannock

County at the northern end of the Shenandoah Valley. Over the four years of the Civil War, armies of both sides had marched, camped, fought over, and devastated the county.

Elias Dodson had an additional problem. One branch of the family was Unionist and the other was so loyal to the Confederacy that they named a son Stonewall Jackson Dodson. After the war, Elias felt it best to leave Virginia, moving west with his wife, Fanny, in the early 1870s. He had since done well with his share of Indiana land.

Like the Messners, the Dodsons believed in education and had sent Maud back to Virginia to school. Maud Messner was a woman of education and social status who, although she never actually worked in the store, became an important figure in its success.

Women were the key to profit in the modern department store. Women might not have been able to vote and their job opportunities were limited, but in the newly middle class America, they had begun to make most of the purchasing decisions.

Maud Messner presided over Saturday night hours at Messner and Son. The lighting was good, the atmosphere was wholesome, and the women of the Oxford area enjoyed a safe and social place to go. The Messners also offered rooms in their building for meetings of the Women's Christian Temperance Union and to the town library. Women felt secure, welcome, and willing to spend.

Dan Messner Junior found himself doing very well indeed. He could afford fine suits, a step up in quality from those sold in the store. When he traveled to New York on buying trips, he visited the wholesalers for store goods and then went to a favorite shoemaker for custom-made footwear, a tailor to make a year's supply of fine cotton shirts, and a favored jeweler for his diamond stickpins.

But still there was the thought of horses. His buying trips allowed him to visit racetracks throughout the Midwest and, occasionally, in the East. Like most sons of Indiana farmers, Dan Messner had little interest in watching Thoroughbreds run, although he could appreciate a fine horse of any breed. What he wanted to see was driving horses, animals who could pull a cart or sulky at a trot almost as fast as other horses could gallop.

Like all sons of Indiana farmers, Messner saw most of his racing at fairs. The fairs were first intended to show off livestock and agricultural products, but by the end of the century the organizers managed to involve the whole family. A farmer might enter his best-looking cow and his plumpest pig, but a housewife from town could also compete for prizes with her favorite quince jam or the embroidered apron that best showed off her needle skills.

Midways began appearing at fairs in the 1870s. The carnival-like rows of tents and booths offered tickets to see bearded women, chances to throw balls and win giant dolls (which nobody ever quite did), and the opportunity to buy sticky, pink candy creams.

Farmers condemned the midway as unwholesome but they were also concerned about competition. Time spent standing in line to see exotic beauties with mustaches or on games you couldn't win anyway was time that couldn't be spent admiring a handsome Jersey bull. But, at county and state fairs of the late nineteenth century, neither the midway nor the livestock competition was the main attraction. The really big crowds came on racing days.

Horse racing, always featuring harness horses rather than runners, qualified as both agriculture and entertainment, even if the farmers with the fine cows grumbled that too much prize money went to the winners of races. Fair organizers realized that while 200 people might watch the class for yearling Guernseys, 2,000 would watch the race for trotters who possessed a two and a half minute record for a mile.

Of the nearly one hundred fairs held across Indiana each year, about half offered racing. Some racing programs consisted of three races on a single afternoon on a makeshift track, while at the bigger fairs the race schedule might include half a dozen races a day for five days over a well-maintained racing surface.

The horses raced almost exclusively at a mile, but a horse had to go several different miles to win a race. During much of the nineteenth century, all American horse racing, running and harness, was conducted in heats. All the entries in a particular race would compete in the first two or three heats, followed by a race off between winners if no one horse won all the heats.

In Thoroughbred racing, heat racing didn't survive the Civil War. Multiple heats in one day were thought to be dangerous to a galloping horse's safety since the gallop is harder on legs and heart than the trot. After four years of war in which more than two million American horses died, nobody wanted to see more killed by sport. By the last quarter of the nineteenth century, almost all runners competed in single race events.

In harness racing, heat competition lasted well into the twentieth century. It disappeared first in ordinary races at small racetracks, until almost all races are now conducted as dashes, or single race events. The sport's most famous event, the Hambletonian, was determined by same-day heats until the mid-1990s. Today there are a few exceptions to the one day, one race policy and even these few are under fire by horsemen who think multiple heats are too stressful.

But heat racing was just fine with Indiana fair-goers like Dan Messner. Heats meant more races and more opportunities to enjoy the horses. And it was primarily a sport for enjoyment. Strictly speaking, betting wasn't even legal in Indiana in the nineteenth century, although nobody pretended that it didn't exist.

When Dan Junior began to go to racetracks, you could wager on races in a few different ways: directly with your friends, with a self-employed bookmaker (if he thought he could get away with it), or, at some fairs, in auction pools. In the pools, more common in the South and East than in the Midwest, the operator wrote tickets for each horse in the race, then sold each ticket to the highest bidder. Holders of winning tickets got the money, minus a cut for the operator.

Dan Messner wasn't known as a betting man, although he made occasional, unrecorded financial support of his opinions in particular races. He attended the fair races with friends from Oxford and neighboring towns, friends with whom he had ongoing discussions about horses. He almost certainly made wagers with them.

John Wattles, Dan Patch's first trainer shown in a 1905 postcard.

Among the friends who went spectating with Messner was John Wattles, reputed to know more about horses than just about anyone else in northwestern Indiana. Wattles was thirty-three years Dan's senior and was both mentor and instructor to the young shopkeeper.

He was also a distant relative by marriage. His wife, Elizabeth Gray Wattles, was sister to the mother-in-law of Dan's older brother, John C. Messner. Wattles owned, trained, and drove racehorses, but seemed unable to convince Dan to take the plunge and get a horse of his own.

Then Dan Messner's nervous stomach struck again. According to a later recollection, abdominal pains sent Dan to the doctor in 1892 or 1893—he couldn't quite remember which.

"There's nothing wrong with you," Messner later recalled the doctor saying. "But you need to get out more. Get a horse, go driving, and get some fresh air."

Dan must have forgotten to tell the doctor about all those trips to the racetrack. Having had the money for some time, he now had the excuse—Dan Messner was going to buy himself a horse. But even with official permission, Messner seemed paralyzed by indecision. He found it excruciatingly difficult to choose a horse.

The ones he liked best—the fast and flashy horses—were, he had to admit, not exactly suitable for leisurely drives in the country.

He even convinced himself that he might find his ideal buggy horse in Lexington, Kentucky, which was already recognized as a wellspring of equine quality. Everything that western Indiana had to support fine horses, central Kentucky had and more. Limestone in the water and the most glorious grass that anybody had ever seen had been luring breeders of fine horses to Lexington since before the Civil War.

Messner traveled repeatedly to Kentucky, supposedly in search of a buggy horse, but usually scheduling his trip when Lexington's famous track was in operation. Unfortunately, the sight of the world's finest horses racing over one of the world's fastest tracks made it more difficult to settle upon a sedate buggy horse. Dan Messner, who could decide in a few minutes on a $2,000 order of coats and shoes and shirtwaists, saw a couple of years go by before he could decide on a $200 driving horse. But indecision turned out to be almost as great a blessing as a nervous stomach.

In the summer of 1894, Dan and a group of friends, John Wattles among them, decided to go to the Remington Fair in Jasper County, Indiana, about thirty miles north of Oxford. The trip took most of the morning, but the Oxford group arrived in time for the fair's final day of racing. When asked about it later, none could remember what happened in any particular race. After the final race, the organizers sponsored an auction of racehorses and breeding stock.

The Oxford friends probably joked about Dan Messner's apocryphal search for a buggy horse, but they agreed to stay for the auction. Messner later claimed that there was nothing about the dark bay mare Zelica that attracted his eye. John Wattles said the same thing when he was asked. Both *were* asked, dozens of times, to explain what it was they noticed, but they never changed their stories. So maybe it was true that Zelica came to Dan Messner by accident—by a glorious stroke of luck.

They certainly wouldn't have noticed Zelica as a result of her racing record. She had lost her only start, pulling up lame. In spite of her youth—she was only three in 1894—her owner believed she would never make a racehorse and apparently subscribed to

Zelica is shown with a later foal. (Photo: International Stock Farm Yearbook 1906)

the theory that only good racehorses make good broodmares. So Zelica was sent to auction.

Today, looking at hundred-year-old photographs of Zelica, you see a compact, attractive horse with good, clean forelegs. Her hind legs may have been set a little too far back, if those old pictures are telling the truth, but she looks like a horse whose original owners should have given a better chance.

Zelica's breeding was certainly worth the second look Messner and Wattles later claimed they never gave her. She had fine horses on both the top and bottom of her pedigree, although an aura of tragedy hung over both sides of the family.

Her sire was a promising, young stallion named Wilkesberry, himself the grandson of the fast, famous, and ill-tempered George Wilkes. George Wilkes was known as the conqueror in 1862 of the great Ethan Allen, the best of the racing trotters of the Morgan breed.

Ethan Allen's defeat represented the beginning of the end of the Morgan as a racehorse, and George Wilkes might have been famous for that alone. But after retiring from the racetrack, he kept up the good work, becoming one of the most celebrated sires of harness race horses in America.

In spite of his impressive pedigree, his grandson Wilkesberry never got a chance to prove himself. He had shown promise with a 2:30 mile (shorthand for two minutes, thirty seconds) and he had sired a handful of good-looking offspring, including the small dark mare named Zelica.

At the age of six, Wilkesberry was being moved to a new barn, tied behind a wagon. The wagon overturned while crossing a stream and Wilkesberry's head was held under water, drowning the gifted, young stallion. His owner knew he had lost something valuable, but he had no idea how great the loss was going to turn out to be.

Zelica's great grandsire on her mother's side, a horse variously known as Abdallah 15 and Alexander's Abdallah, is at the same time among the most important and most tragic figures in the history of his sport. If Wilkesberry's death resulted from human stupidity, Abdallah's epitomized cruelty.

Abdallah was a horse who pleased the eye from the moment he was born. Owner Lewis Sutton, a horse broker from Orange County, New York, didn't expect much of his colt, whose mother was a lame mare of unknown pedigree. But his expectations soared as soon as he saw the colt in action.

He was a perfectly shaped, young animal, a fact that was impressive enough to a man looking to make a profit on a horse. But more important to the horsemen of Orange County, New York, the colt could trot.

The county was a seedbed for fast harness horses, and a horse who could stay on a trot even as a baby was something everybody wanted. If he didn't gallop as a baby, he probably wouldn't do it while pulling a cart either. The word soon got out that Sutton's new colt would follow his mother in the pasture at the best looking trot you'd ever seen.

You couldn't scare the colt out of a trot on a bet. People would converge on the Sutton pasture and try to make the young colt gallop. They would shout, clap hands, occasionally even shoot a gun. Still, the colt trotted. What's more, startled by all the noise, the colt trotted faster.

The word spread that Lewis Sutton had a little trotting machine and the colt became the object of desire of one of the most important breeders in the Hudson Valley. When Seeley Edsall arrived at the Sutton farm to take a look at the young marvel, he couldn't resist trying to do what so many others had failed at. He brought a large sheepdog, which he sent chasing after the colt. The colt trotted. In 1854, Edsall bought the almost two-year-old colt, giving Sutton a handsome profit on a baby produced from a worthless mare.

Edsall expected a great deal from the colt. Beyond the impeccable trot, there were the good looks. He was a small, dark bay horse with the head of a blue blooded Thoroughbred. His delicate muzzle, people said, was so tiny that he "could have taken a drink out of a pint cup." It was a description often used of Arabians, but rarely of trotting horses.

In spite of his trotting ability, Edsall decided not to race his colt, although he was willing to demonstrate the horse's magnificent gait whenever asked. He felt that the beautiful colt, whom he named Edsall's Hambletonian, could only hurt his reputation if he appeared on the racetrack. Unraced, he could always be a horse of infinite promise.

The plan worked, and hundreds of owners from around New York State were willing to pay $25 to breed their mares to the young stallion. In 1859, before many of his nearly 200 New York offspring reached the racetrack, Edsall's Hambletonian was sold for the substantial price of $2,500 and taken to Kentucky.

When he arrived in Cynthiana, Kentucky, stories of his extraordinary appearance preceded him. He was trotted at full speed down the main street as hundreds of onlookers cheered, and most agreed that they had never seen a horse trot so fast.

Renamed Abdallah, he became one of the most important trotting stallions in Kentucky.

The four years of Civil War were hard on the horses of Central Kentucky. The Union cavalry confiscated some, although officers were usually willing to respect valuable breeding stock. Confederates, hungrier for mounts, were sometimes less careful.

Kentucky was a border state, officially loyal to the Union but filled with Confederate sympathizers. Union armies gained control of the area around Lexington early in the war, but Confederate raiders, mostly under the command of Lexington native John Hunt Morgan, made repeated forays into the heart of the Bluegrass. Hunt's admirers called him the "Thunderbolt of the Confederacy," while Union loyalists preferred "that damn horse thief." The danger to your horses depended on where your sympathies lay.

Abdallah's owner, Robert Alexander, tried to make sure that his sympathies lay directly in the middle. As a British subject, he believed that both sides would respect the horses on his 3,200-acre Woodburn Stud, the largest horse farm in North America. In addition to Abdallah, Woodburn was home to America's most important Thoroughbred stallion of the nineteenth century—Lexington. Alexander had paid $15,000 for Lexington in 1856, a record price for a horse of any breed.

Alexander's faith in the protection of his citizenship led him to keep most of his horses in place at Woodburn while other owners sent their animals north of the Ohio River. Union troops left them alone, and Morgan, who believed himself to be a man of honor, never permitted a Woodburn horse to be taken. With the exception of one young horse who was quickly ransomed, the Alexander band remained intact.

By the beginning of 1865, with war's end in sight, other breeders began to bringing their horses home. On February 2, a raiding partly of Confederates swept through the Lexington area, snatching horses and robbing citizens. Among the horses seized were fifteen owned by a shocked Robert Alexander. One of the stolen horses was Abdallah.

Alexander and the others had never felt threatened by John Morgan who was, after all, one of them. But the dashing Morgan was now six months dead, shot in the back along a road in Tennessee, betrayed, everyone said, by a woman. These raiders were followers of William Quantrill, a homicidal marauder whom even the desperate Confederate army had disavowed.

Abdallah, unshod and unused to being ridden, was driven to the point of death by his captor. He was abandoned about twenty miles from home, where he died shortly after Union army rescuers found him. In a classic case of closing the barn door after the horses were out, Alexander sent the remainder of his best horses north into Ohio for the last two months of the war.

Abdallah was only twelve at the time of his death, but his influence on his sport has been so great that the majority of fast harness horses today descend from him. His dominance was not as prevalent in 1894, fewer than thirty years after his death, but his name in a pedigree signaled quality.

We don't know if Dan Messner and his friends looked closely enough at Zelica's pedigree to notice Abdallah's name in it. Probably not, if they really weren't paying attention to the small, dark mare. Maybe, if they were thinking about where she got her good looks.

Years later, Messner related the story of the auction to the *Oxford Tribune,* and it's not clear whether he was trying to appear modest, lucky, prescient, or all three. After several forgettable horses were led through the ring, the pretty little daughter of Wilkesberry was announced by the auctioneer. He told the crowd that he had received a telegraphed bid of $250 for her. If he couldn't get $255 from the Indiana audience, the auctioneer said, she was off to New York.

The auction attendees might have wondered why a mare with such a limited racing record would draw a respectable bid from halfway across the country, but the puzzlement prompted nobody to offer his own bid. Just as the auctioneer was about to sell Zelica to the telegraphed bid, Messner—according to his later memory—nodded to an acquaintance he just happened to spot on the other side of the ring.

"Sold!" said the auctioneer, pointing his hammer towards Dan Messner, who agreed to take the mare rather than claim a mistake by the auctioneer. So for $255, a middling price for a young mare with respectable breeding, Dan Messner had himself a horse.

Messner later claimed that his friends teased him mercilessly about his accidental purchase, but it's hard to believe that an astute horseman like old John Wattles would not have seen a little something in Zelica. As he made arrangements to have Zelica transported to Oxford, Messner may have felt a twinge of concern about buying a lame mare when he really needed a buggy horse. Or he may have been pleased with the transaction. But there's no way he could have known that his $255 bank draft represented one of the shrewdest purchases in the history of the sport he had grown to love.

3

MR. MESSNER'S BUGGY HORSE

THROUGH THE FALL and winter, Dan Messner drove Zelica through Oxford in front of a newly purchased buggy. A four-wheeled box on springs, the buggy was the vehicle of choice for most people in late nineteenth century America. Although nobody now alive in Oxford is old enough to remember Messner driving his sprightly runabout buggy and his new mare, some of their grandparents and great-grandparents did.

They passed down the story of handsome young Dan Messner, the pretty mare who was reputed to be lame but looked lively enough, and the pleasure both showed in their daily jaunts. Messner talked about the circumstances of his purchase, suggesting that the joke was on him, but he relished the admiring glances his new horse drew.

Zelica may not have been much of a racehorse, but she was an attractive animal of obvious quality and some people suspected that Messner's bid might not have been such an accident after all. The underbidder at Remington had been Harry Haws of Pennsylvania, a young man who had inherited a valuable brick works. He was, according to his biography, "interested in all wholesome and elevating sports." He was known to be on the lookout for good racehorses and breeding stock.

Messner and friends spent hours talking in Kelley's Livery, the largest stable in Oxford, with its 3,600 square feet of stalls and vehicle storage space. It stood north of the town square, a walk of five minutes from the Messner store. Dan Messner sometimes kept Zelica in a small barn behind his home, but he often boarded her at Kelley's for equine and human companionship.

There is no modern equivalent to the livery stable in its importance in small town life. In additional to boarding horses and selling feed and equipment to horse owners, a livery offered horses and vehicles of all kinds for rent by the day or hour. You could rent a hooded surrey for a two-hour spin with your best girl, a four-horse wagon to transport your household goods, or a shiny black hearse should one unfortunately be needed.

Even in a comfortable town like Oxford, most people didn't keep horses. For travel about town, they could walk. For longer distances, they could buy a reasonably priced ticket on one of the half dozen trains that stopped in Oxford each day. When they did need a vehicle, they turned to establishments like Kelley's.

Livery stables were vital to travelers, especially the traveling salesmen who had goods to show and deliver, and Kelley's location across from the Ohio House Hotel and near the railway depots brought daily customers. But the importance of livery stables, Kelley's included, went well beyond transportation.

It was a gathering place for men, more respectable than a tavern, where you could learn something important if you wanted to and usually go home sober besides. Horses were essential, even to people who preferred not to own them, and in a livery stable you could find experts to answer questions, to tell you stories about great horses of the past, and to assure you that you'd made a good purchase. Or not, as the case may be.

William Kelley himself knew a lot about horses, but, as far as Dan Messner was concerned, the real expert was among Kelley's customers: John Wattles. He had listened to Wattles's advice and stories for years, at least since his brother had married into the Wattles family. Now, sitting around the coal stove at Kelley's with Zelica just down the shed row, Messner had particular reason to listen.

Wattles, sixty-eight years old that winter, had farmed two hundred acres northwest of Oxford for forty years. He still owned the farm, but he had built a house and barn in town the previous year and now concentrated on his small string of racehorses.

John Wattles, who with his flowing gray beard looked a little like an Old Testament prophet, had added to his reputation in Oxford in 1892 with the success of his trotting colt Cottonwood—a horse he bred, trained, and drove. Not only had Cottonwood won several races at fairs in Illinois and Indiana, he had brought in nearly $1,000 in a private sale at the end of the racing season.

Now, in the spring of 1895, John Wattles and Dan Messner discussed what to do about Zelica. They maintained the fiction

Joe Patchen shown in 1895, when he was first bred to Zelica. *(Photo: Scribner's Magazine June 1896)*

that her purchase had been an accident and that Messner was satisfied to use her as a buggy horse, but their long-running discussions suggested that the truth lay elsewhere.

In May, Messner decided, with Wattles' urging, to take Zelica to Chebanse, Illinois, forty miles from Oxford. In exchange for a $150 stud fee, she was bred to the great pacer Joe Patchen during his first season at stud. Wattles demonstrated the courage of his convictions by paying the fee for his own mare, Oxford Girl.

A month later, after being pronounced in foal, Zelica returned to Oxford and to her pleasant life as a buggy horse. But the little mare with no racing record to speak of was now a $405 horse, and by 1895 standards she had become high priced transportation.

That summer, Messner liked to joke that he had made the worst of a bad buy when he spent the money on Joe Patchen's hefty stud fee, but both he and Wattles probably suspected they had made a good choice. Yes, it was a lot of money, they would acknowledge, but Joe Patchen was a lot of horse—one of the best racehorses in the country and surely the most popular in the Midwest. To those who claimed that nothing in Zelica's race record merited such an expenditure, they could respond that the history of harness racing was filled with horses whose mothers were not just unproven but unknown. Zelica, at least, had a decent pedigree.

At first glance, the Joe Patchen mating was risky, and not just financially. Zelica's sire, Wilkesberry, was a grandson of George Wilkes, as was Joe Patchen. The relationship between the two wasn't considered incestuous in those days, but there was concern that the foal might inherit George Wilkes's tempestuous nature. Of course, it might just as easily inherit his considerable speed.

In one way, the match was ideal. To students of pedigree, Joe Patchen and Zelica might well produce an ideal pacing race-horse, a horse with a perfect pacing gait plus the speed of the best running horses, and that wasn't easy to find.

Pacing horses aren't the only members of the animal world who utilize their unusual gait at the intermediate speed between walking and running, but the majority of four-legged animals prefer the two-beat, diagonal trot. In the trot, legs on the corners of the body move forward in unison. As the left front goes forward, so does the right back, followed by the right front and back left. It's an efficient, well-balanced way to get where you're going if you happen to have four legs.

Cats trot, as do sheep, goats, wolves, raccoons, elephants, and most dogs. If a human being gets down on his hands and knees, he will use the trot pattern, although only year-olds can do it at anything approaching speed.

The pacing gait, in which legs on each side of the body move in unison, is faster than the trot. *(Drawing: International Stock Food Farm Yearbook 1906)*

The pace, also a two-beat gait, is lateral rather than diagonal. The left front and left rear legs move forward together as the right front and right rear move back. For a creature with four legs, it can appear to be an awkward, unbalanced way of going.

Some pacing animals look like they might topple over at any moment. Camels, giraffes, and an East African antelope called the gerenuk pace rather than trot, and only the gerenuk could be said to have a graceful gait. The pacing gait is not a conscious choice among these animals. It's simply the way members of these species move.

Other animals pace, although they're not really supposed to. Dogs, especially big, old, or lame ones, often shift to a pace to reduce stress on backs or joints. It's called a "fatigue gait" in dogs and is almost never acceptable in the show ring. One exception: The Olde English Sheep Dog is permitted an amble or pace when moving slowly.

The horse is a little different from camels, sheep dogs, or tired German Shepherds. A great majority of them trot, including all members of most breeds. But horses of certain breeds pace or perform a gait, sometimes a four-beat one, similar to the pace. Icelandic ponies, American Saddlebreds, Tennessee Walking Horses, Missouri Fox Trotters, Paso Finos and their cousins the Peruvian Pasos, and others are considered gaited horses, and that gait (sometimes more than one gait) resembles the pace.

Those breeds are relatively new, but the pace is not. A few of the horses in the prehistoric cave art in Lascaux, France, demonstrate an identifiable pace.

The oldest portrayal of a domesticated horse using a pacing gait is a nearly 3,000-year-old bas-relief sculpture from ancient

Babylon. The very earliest illustrations from Geoffrey Chaucer's *Canterbury Tales,* written in the late 1300s, show several pilgrims, including the Wife of Bath, riding pacers. The ambler, as the laterally gaited horse was called, spent centuries as the most popular casual riding horse in the world. The gait was considered more comfortable to ride, although trotters were preferred for pulling vehicles.

The reputation for comfort was most likely because poor roads meant that nobody went fast on horseback. A slow ambling gait is indeed comfortable to ride, a little like gentle side-to-side rocking, while a fast one can cause something nearer to sideways whiplash. Once roads improved and speed became possible, preference switched to trotters, whose middle gait could be made comfortable by rising or "posting" to the diagonal beat. You can't post to a pacer, who has no diagonal.

But how did we get from the Wife of Bath's petite ambler—wending her way to Canterbury in 1370—to another pretty, little pacing horse pulling a buggy around Oxford, Indiana, in 1895? That is one of history's mysteries.

We know the source of Zelica's pace in terms of her immediate American ancestors, but how the gait got to Indiana was a subject of endless speculation. It may even have been discussed around the coal stove at William Kelley's livery. Most of the men would have given credit to the Canadian pacers who came down to Tennessee earlier in the century, but some of them may have wanted to know why those Canadian horses paced in the first place.

Although there is debate, the pace probably traveled to Canada from the United States in the form of descendants of Narragansett Pacers. The Narragansett first appeared as an identifiable breed in the late 1600s in Rhode Island, a colony created as a plantation for religious iconoclasts but soon transformed into the center of colonial American seafaring.

Legend had it that the Narragansett breed developed from a handsome Andalusian stallion rescued from the sea off the coast of Spain by a Rhode Island ship captain, never mind that Andalusians don't pace. A couple of Spanish breeds did, so it was a believable story, especially given the seafaring nature of the region. Unfortunately for the owners of Narragansetts, who enjoyed believing that their animals were the descendants of a magnificent Spanish stallion, the probable truth was somewhat less dramatic.

During the 300 years between the Canterbury pilgrims and the ones who settled New England, the British pacing horse was alive and well, living under new names in rural Scotland and Ireland. The Galloway of Scotland and the Hobbie (yes, the living version of the hobby horse) of Ireland were small, easy-riding, pacing horses. Given the constant ship commerce between Britain and its American colonies, some undoubtedly had arrived by the middle of the seventeenth century. The small stature and comfortable gait of the Galloways and Hobbies made them ideal for the narrow paths through thick American woodlands. A little cross breeding for size produced the Narragansett Pacer.

A Scottish horseman, describing Narragansetts for an audience back home, said they were "the finest saddle horses in the world. They pace naturally and with such swiftness and for so long . . . as must appear almost incredible to those who have not experienced it."

Narragansetts were mostly bright chestnut, gleaming shades of gold and red, and they usually sported white on the face and legs. They were not particularly beautiful, but they were unusually fast at their pacing gait and that led to racing as soon as Puritan sensibilities allowed. In the 1720s results of the first pacing races in America appear in the records. The horses in these races were ridden, not driven in front of vehicles.

George Washington, as a Virginia aristocrat, was used to the best in horseflesh and was the proud owner of a racing Narragansett. Washington's diary mentions an appearance by his racehorse in 1768, when he presumably still had time for sport, seven years before the start of the American Revolution. At least one Narragansett actually played a role in the Revolution. A fast mare, assumed to be a Narragansett by her description, carried Paul Revere with his warning to Lexington and Concord.

But in spite of the admiration of the Founding Fathers, the Narragansett Pacer didn't long survive the Revolution. It's not clear why, but it probably had something to do with prosperity. Better roads meant that wagons and carriages were now practical, and large trotting horses were more suited to pulling them.

What's more, American farmers of the post-Revolution years had enough time and enough education to try a little purpose-breeding. Do you like the speed and the quality of the Narragansett but want a little more size? Breed your pacing mare to a draft stallion. Would you prefer a trotter to a pacer, even though you like everything else about your Narragansett? Just pick a trotting mate, and nine out of ten times you'll get a trotter.

The Narragansett Pacer's quality worked against his survival as a breed. By the last few years of the eighteenth century, even his greatest admirers realized that they had bred their pacers to members of too many different breeds. One Narragansett stallion owner offered a greatly reduced stud fee for any full-blooded Narragansett mare, hoping, he said, to save the breed. It apparently didn't work. A few years later, the owner of a Connecticut stallion was able to advertise his horse as the last full-blooded Narragansett available for breeding.

Although the last Narragansett Pacer was gone by 1820, his blood survived and prospered. As the Narragansett disappeared, the Morgan emerged as the most important horse of the Northeast. The father of the breed, a mostly Thoroughbred horse eventually named Justin Morgan after his owner, probably had no Narragansett blood himself. But, although a trotter, he may have been partly responsible for the survival of the pacing gait in North America.

Justin Morgan, foaled about 1788 in Massachusetts, made his name in neighboring Vermont. He was acknowledged within a radius of fifty or so miles of his home in Randolph as a useful little horse, comfortable to ride, sturdy enough for farm work, fast in running races, cooperative, gentle, and modestly good looking.

But there was something different about Justin Morgan. He, with hardly an exception, sired offspring that looked and behaved almost exactly like him. Mare owners handed over their few dollars, not so much because they expected spectacular foals, but because they were virtually guaranteed sturdy, good-gaited, hard-working, and pleasant-natured colts and fillies. They paid the fee for their Canadian draft mares, their part Thoroughbred mares, their ponies of indecipherable lineage. They discovered that their full- or half-blooded Narragansett Pacer mares made a perfect match with Justin Morgan.

Hundreds of Morgan horses were sold across the border into Quebec, where they were bred to local horses of English and Dutch ancestry. These were primarily trotting horses, when they could be urged into a gait as fast as a trot, and to some observers their finest quality was that they were what horsemen call "easy keepers." That's a good thing in a climate where grass grows for only part of the year.

Crossed with these horses, the Morgans produced a substantial percentage of pacers. Although few records were kept, Canadian horse buyers of the early nineteenth century probably also imported a few horses with a larger percentage of Narragansett blood and may have had some of the English and Irish amblers. The result of all this importation and crossbreeding was the Canadian Pacer, a horse appreciated for being good-gaited, sturdy, and still an easy keeper. These horses who came to the pace in a rather random way became the ancestors of Tennessee Walking Horses, American Saddlebreds, Missouri Fox Trotters, and a few other breeds who either prefer or can be taught to use the pace.

In addition to the pacing gait, something else popped up in the Morgan-Narragansett-English crosses who headed south and west into the United States. That was the swiftness so much admired by Paul Revere and George Washington in the Narragansett and so remarked upon by the farmers who bred their mares to Justin Morgan. Racing seemed inevitable.

But there was one problem. Racing at a speed less than a gallop, now conducted with horses under harness rather than saddle, was widespread, lucrative, well publicized, and popular during the middle of the nineteenth century. But it was almost exclusively the province of trotting horses.

The successful ones were household names: Lady Suffolk, Flora Temple, Goldsmith Maid, Ethan Allen, and Dexter. They, more than the running Thoroughbreds, were beloved by fans and immortalized by lithographers like Currier and Ives. All were admired for their rapid, elegant, extravagant trots.

The moneyed patrons of the sport went beyond simply preferring trotters. William Vanderbilt, heir to the already famous fortune, spent thousands on trotters for racing and driving but declared he wouldn't have a pacer in his stable at any price. Robert Bonner, a New York publisher and sportsman who paid Vanderbilt $40,000 for his aging trotting mare Maud S. in 1884, avowed, "No gentleman drives a pacer."

Gentlemen might not, but Midwestern farmers would. They refused to share the prejudice against pacers, which (they felt) existed for some pretty foolish reasons. First was the appearance of the gait. The very act of moving legs on one side of the body forward and back at the same time made the pacer look stiff in the knee. Most also appeared to swing their legs wide as they moved, leading to the uncomplimentary name of "sidewheeler."

Then there was the appearance of the horse himself. Pacers tended to be too short in the body, too long in the head, and too hairy (thanks to those cold Vermont and Canadian winters). All in all, not an appealing package, except of course for all that speed.

Midwesterners, already known by mid-century for their appreciation of the homely virtues, overlooked appearance and concentrated instead on speed. They supported paces appearing on the same programs as trots. There weren't as many paces as trots, but

The pacing-bred pacer Star Pointer was the first two-minute harness racehorse. *(Photo: International Stock Food Farm Yearbook 1906)*

at least there were some to enjoy. It also made obvious the fact considered embarrassing to the trotting enthusiasts. Pacers were faster than trotters.

The first harness racing horse to notch a 2:30 second mile was a pacer, Aggie Down. A pacer was the first 2:25 harness horse, the pacer Pet was the first horse to go 2:20, and so on right down the line to the pacer Star Pointer, who was the first two minute miler in the sport. Midwesterners saw no reason to look down their noses at pacers, even if what they were looking at wasn't particularly handsome.

These milestone makers were descendants of pacers brought from Canada, pacers who emerged in Indiana and Kentucky and

Tennessee, and pacers who appeared mysteriously in front of carts and wagons. There was Copperbottom, who arrived in Kentucky in 1816 and was reputed to be from Canada. There was Tom Hal, who showed up in Kentucky in 1824 and was also said to be Canadian. There was Pilot, who appeared as a peddler's horse in New Orleans in 1831 and might have been from anywhere.

Each of these pacing stallions became the father, grandfather, and great-grandfather of fast pacing racehorses. Mr. Vanderbilt probably knew none of their names, but Indiana and the rest of the Midwest certainly did.

Pacing began to get attention elsewhere in the late 1870s, not because of the speed of the horses but because of heated

The trotter Hambletonian was the ancestor of the modern Standardbred, trotter and pacer alike. (Lithograph: Currier and Ives)

competition among a group of appealing pacers. Two mares, named Lucy and Mattie Hunter, and two stallions, Rowdy Boy and Sleepy Tom, plus a few other fine horses, pushed each other to impressive wins and even more impressive times.

Sleepy Tom was a particular favorite of Midwestern racing fans. He was blind and relied on the voice of his driver to direct him. When he paced the fastest mile in history in July 1879, not incidentally a full second faster than the best ever by a trotter, a pacer finally became nationally famous. But even Sleepy Tom wasn't entirely respected. He was sold for $6,000 after his record mile, a fraction of what a top trotter would bring.

There were more great pacing horses who emerged in the last decades of the nineteenth century, including the fastest of them all, Star Pointer. When this descendant of Tom Hal set his record of 1:59¼ at Readville, Massachusetts, in 1897, the sport's Holy Grail—the two-minute mile—had been found.

Lovers of fast pacers hoped that Star Pointer's glory would lead to acceptance and popularity for their favorites. Breeders and owners of pacers also hoped for bigger purses and higher sales prices. It indeed happened, although it wasn't Star Pointer but rather the horses he defeated on his way to his milestone that prompted the change in attitude.

Astute observers suspected that Star Pointer might be an equine dinosaur. He descended, as well as anybody could figure his pedigree, exclusively from the pacing horses who had appeared in the Midwest in the early to mid-nineteenth century. He was a strong, sturdy horse with a big, plain head. Star Pointer looked like a working horse whose ancestors had pulled rocks from fields in Vermont and had survived Quebec winters.

His two greatest rivals were instead direct descendants of a little New York stallion who was mostly Thoroughbred. Hambletonian was a great-grandson of the fine English Thoroughbred Messenger, imported to America in 1788. Hambletonian himself was born in 1849 and was known from an early age as an outstanding trotter. He never raced, although he was exhibited at his beautiful trotting gait to encourage owners to breed their mares to him.

This they did, and by the end of the nineteenth century nearly every successful harness racehorse descended from him. Not just almost every successful trotter, but almost every pacer also featured Hambletonian in his pedigree. They were all considered trotting-bred—pacers included. Hambletonian appears as the direct male line ancestor of both Joe Patchen and Zelica, making their offspring doubly a trotting-bred pacer.

In one sense, some of the pacers remained trotters. Many of them actually trotted when left to their own devices in a pasture, and some even trotted when hitched to a non-racing vehicle like Dan Messner's buggy. Even today, more than 150 years after the birth of Hambletonian, some of his pacing descendants prefer to trot and they pace only in competition or training. Others pace and do nothing but pace.

So why did the Hambletonian pacers pace? A look at the meticulously kept records of Hambletonian's mates shows several whose mothers had unknown breeding and may have been Canadian or other pacers. His own mother, known only as the Charles Kent Mare, was the daughter of Bellfounder, an English coaching stallion. Some of his ancestors were known to produce "amblers."

It's also possible that the Thoroughbred blood of Hambletonian contributed to the gait. His great-great-grandsire Mambrino, who never left England, was himself a descendant of a prominent English racehorse named Bald Galloway, who appears in many Thoroughbred pedigrees, even today. The name "Galloway" could well mean that this horse was a pacer.

Most of the other Hambletonians were trotters, and the fact that both gaits were coming from the same source assured that pacers were included when the harness racing community established "The Standard," a rulebook that created a new harness racing breed. The 1879 guideline determined that any horse who could go a mile in 2:30 or better or was the offspring of 2:30 horses would qualify as Standardbred. Pacers were required to go 2:25. Not surprisingly, plenty of pacers were at the top of the list when pedigree papers were handed out.

Dan Messner continued using Zelica, whether at the pace or trot in her casual usage, through the summer and fall of 1895. He probably stopped driving when the streets of Oxford became icy, although there was no reason to keep her inside on dry days. A young mare, a first-time mother, would probably not show much until the eight or nine month mark of her eleven month gestation, and even then a growing belly wouldn't stop her usefulness until perhaps the final month. Zelica, with her Joe Patchen foal inside her, was valuable. Messner, while he would not have worried about the danger of light work, would have been reluctant to risk injury to her if the going was less than perfect.

Today, valuable broodmares of the racing breeds rarely do work of any kind, even early in their pregnancies. But horsemen of the nineteenth century knew that mares who remain in use during pregnancy not only don't suffer, they foal more easily. So Zelica reached the spring of 1896 in good health, sound, and ready to show Oxford what a $150 foal looked like.

Left to their own devices, mares will choose to give birth outside, in the middle of the night, with neither horse nor human for company. Zelica wasn't given that choice. As her due date approached, she was confined to her stall at Kelley's.

The livery stable was a regular stop for Dr. A. B. Carter, a veterinarian who diagnosed illnesses and performed equine surgery every Wednesday and Friday. Another veterinary surgeon practiced in Oxford as well, and William Kelley himself lived next door to the stable. Zelica was well watched. They, and John Wattles too, were experienced enough to notice the subtle signs of impending birth in late April. Two days before the end of the month, a swelling udder, loosening of the muscles below the tail, and Zelica's increasing restlessness told them the Joe Patchen foal was on its way.

In the end, Zelica did it all by herself. In the early morning of April 29, 1896, with no trouble to speak of, she produced a large dark colt. Messner, Kelley, Wattles, and other lovers of fine horses hurried to the livery stable to see him.

A later legend, an effort to create the most basic kind of rags-to-riches story, claimed that Zelica foaled in a pile of manure. If so, it was manure she had recently produced, because William Kelley prided himself on the quality of his operation. If the legend was designed to show that Zelica's colt had an unpromising start to his life, truth should have been enough.

The truth was that Zelica's high-priced, eagerly awaited colt looked terrible. It would be a blessing, some of the observers thought, if he didn't survive the night.

4

MESSNER'S FOLLY

NO JUST-BORN FOAL looks good. His head is too big for his body, his legs are too long for his height, his ears are flat, and he comes out all wet. The men who gazed down on Zelica's colt, who lay sprawled next to his mother in the straw of her stall, were experienced enough to know that. Even so, this foal seemed particularly bad to each of them.

William Kelley was first to see him in the early morning hours of April 29, followed by Dan Messner, who came immediately when summoned. Both were terribly disappointed in what they saw: a dark colt, thin even for a newborn, with excessively knobby knees and crooked legs. Messner later said that his dreams of racing success with the Joe Patchen colt ended at that moment. "I honestly thought he would never do anything but pull a delivery wagon," he added.

Even that future seemed unlikely when Kelley and Messner realized that the colt wasn't able to stand to nurse from Zelica, who had scrambled to her feet within minutes of giving birth. The moment of first nursing is critical in the life of a young horse, so important that nowadays most stud fees aren't payable to the stallion owner until the foal stands and takes milk from his mother. You don't owe the money when the mare conceives, not even when she delivers a live foal. No, it's not due until that foal gets up and nurses from its dam.

First nursing is important beyond the nourishment it provides. The composition of the mare's initial milk is vital to the survival of her foal. The colostrum, as it's called, contains both antibodies to protect the baby from disease and a chemical compound that helps the digestive system start working.

A foal has two hours, three at most, to nurse from its mother. After that, its chances of long-term survival are dramatically reduced even though it can be fed cow's milk. Messner, not yet ready to give up on the odd-looking colt, decided against letting nature take its course. As William Kelley watched over mare and foal, Messner went outside to look for help.

Driving down North Howard Street in a wagon pulled by a two-horse team was Messner's friend Ancil Beecher Gwin, who was summoned inside to assist. The eagerly awaited Joe Patchen colt had arrived, Messner told Gwin, but his legs were so crooked that he couldn't stand up.

Messner, Kelley, and Gwin managed to support the colt long enough for him to nurse, while other Oxford horse lovers, having heard about the birth, crowded around the stall. The verdict was universal: The mating of Joe Patchen and Zelica was a high-priced failure. A disaster, even.

John Wattles was especially disappointed, and not just because his advice now seemed so bad. His own mare was about to give birth to a Joe Patchen foal herself and that prospect had lost some of its luster.

Later, there were a lot of stories about that first morning, probably more stories than the number of people who could possibly have been there. The stories were consistent. One man suggested that the foal be knocked in the head so it wouldn't suffer. Another predicted that the colt wouldn't live, even if he weren't hurried along to death. Nobody claimed later to have seen any promise in Zelica's dark bay colt. He was immediately given a nickname: Messner's Folly.

He wasn't knocked in the head and he did live. After two days of human assistance, the crooked legs proved strong enough to bear the colt's weight. Zelica turned out to be a good milk producer and the colt grew rapidly, filling out just the way a healthy foal should.

Signs of racing potential in the colt remained elusive, no matter how hard Dan Messner might look. But people did start noticing something about Zelica's baby. He might not have the conformation to become a racehorse, they noted, but he certainly had the personality to become a favorite pet. He was alert, cheerful, and totally unafraid of human beings.

Zelica herself was known throughout Oxford for her gentle and friendly nature, looking for treats from everybody who stopped Dan Messner for a conversation. Too bad, people said, that the colt seemed to have inherited both his personality and his racing potential from his mother. Joe Patchen's talent was nowhere to be seen.

But a few people thought there was a little something that might have come from the Iron Horse, although they acknowledged it might be wishful thinking. Zelica's Joe Patchen colt looked uncommonly intelligent. The big dark eyes closely observed all the people who came to visit and seemed to remember them.

A week or so after the foaling, Zelica and her son were moved to John Wattles's farm northwest of Oxford, where they could be turned out to graze. It's tempting with a cherished foal, particularly one with a weakness, to keep him safely closed up in a stall rather than risk him outdoors. But being outside, running to catch up with his mother, looking for the most tender blades of grass, is crucial to his physical and psychological development.

After a few weeks at the Wattles farm, the colt's conformation somehow didn't look so bad anymore. Only one of the legs, the left hind, still looked dreadful, and his foal coat of indeterminate dark brown had begun to sleek into a beautiful mahogany bay. What's more, almost everybody could now see that the intelligence was real.

There were other mares and foals on the farm, including the Joe Patchen foal owned by John Wattles, who had turned out to be a bay filly. Years later, even with the benefit of hindsight, nobody claimed they had observed racing talent in Zelica's colt as he played with the other foals. Some even admitted that they thought he was the most awkward of the group.

But they did notice that the dark colt was inventive and mischievous in his games, keeping his companions guessing about what he might do. Part of what made Joe Patchen a great racehorse was his intelligence—his understanding of what it meant to win and what might be necessary to make that happen. Yes, Zelica's colt might have inherited a little something from his sire after all.

At some point during the summer, Zelica resumed her work as a buggy horse. She and her colt alternated between the farm and the Messner barn in town. The colt was usually allowed to run alongside his mother as she was driven and had no trouble keeping up with her. Dan Messner began to think he might have a decent buggy horse, thereby recouping some of his investment.

Charles Maguire, Dan Messner's sixteen-year-old groom, was the first person to see that the colt might aspire to something more than a life as a buggy horse, although he later claimed he didn't pay much attention to it at the time. Maguire, known in Oxford as Mickey, was responsible for seeing that Zelica was able to graze while she was stabled at Messner's in-town barn.

In an interview given decades later, Mickey described how he would lead Zelica with halter and rope while her free-headed foal danced behind her as they headed out to pastures or roadside grass. The colt quickly discovered a great game: If he dashed off while his mother grazed, his teenaged handler would be forced to run to catch him.

Years later, as an elderly man, Mickey Maguire recounted the story of the day he decided to teach Zelica's impish baby a lesson. They were on a road heading east out of Oxford when he stopped to allow the mare to graze on the roadside. As usual, the colt bounced and darted further and further away, finally reaching a point more than half a mile ahead of his mother and handler.

But this time, instead of chasing down the little adventurer, the young groom turned Zelica and headed back towards town. The colt, horrified at the prospect of losing his mother, wheeled around and dashed after them, closing the distance so quickly that Mickey was stunned. At the time, Mickey Maguire found it more amusing than portentous, but later he said it was that moment he knew Zelica's dark bay colt might actually amount to something.

Under normal circumstances, Zelica and her foal would have been separated sometime around October 1896. Weaning, then as today, usually happens when the foal is five to six months of age. At that age, a young horse can eat everything it needs to maintain itself. The mare, after carrying a fetus for eleven months and feeding a baby for five, usually needs a break. Because of tight quarters in the Messner barn, the weaning may have come later. With Zelica and her baby, nobody thought it important to note the time and circumstances since weaning is not a significant moment in the life of a buggy horse.

Any domestic horse's first lessons really begin within moments of birth. Even if he doesn't need help, as Zelica's foal did, he will be handled and touched. Over the next several months, his feet will be lifted and examined, although he usually won't need trimming or shoeing for a few months more. Better to familiarize him with standing on three feet while he's still small enough to control.

Most young horses are taught to wear halters or rope head collars during the first few weeks of their lives. Some people prefer not to halter very young horses, since there's a slight but distinct danger that an investigative hoof can find itself caught. Dan Messner was apparently a believer in controlling a foal by controlling its mother, and the people of Oxford enjoyed the sight of Zelica's baby happily following along without being forced.

After weaning, with the mother no longer hovering protectively, training becomes more intense. During the fall of 1896, Zelica's son would have learned to be led with halter and rope. He may have had the horny growth of his hooves trimmed for the first time at one of the blacksmith's shops in Oxford, but it's unlikely that he would have been shod for his weanling lessons.

Sometime over the colt's first winter, Dan Messner and John Wattles decided that there might be some reason to give him a

Joe Patchen, on the right, became one of the country's best pacers in the last years of the nineteenth century. *(Lithograph: Currier and Ives)*

chance as a racehorse. In all the interviews Messner did later, he never said exactly what he had begun to see in his dark bay colt. Other people remembered the colt as still having bad legs as he approached his first birthday. But the rest of him was beautiful and he had learned his early lessons with grace and enthusiasm.

Most likely, Messner and Wattles went over the pedigree again, and they saw the reason they had sent Zelica to Joe Patchen in the first place. The colt was well bred and, in the absence of a race record, breeding was the best available predictor of a young horse's racing potential. In the case of Zelica's dark colt, the potential that was so dim in person was still bright and clear on paper.

In fact, the breeding had actually improved in the nearly two years since Zelica had made the trip to Illinois. Joe Patchen had emerged as one of the best pacing horses in history during the summer of 1896, the months following the birth of his first crop of foals. His stud fee had increased and his offspring were in great demand, even though none was yet old enough to race.

Wattles may have had more hope for his own Joe Patchen foal, the bay filly who had raced in the pastures with Zelica's baby. He had named her Joan Patchen, and everyone in Oxford felt she had a chance to be a good racer. Messner was probably a little less optimistic about his colt, but he asked Wattles to try him out anyway. Poor conformation was no guarantee of poor performance, even if it didn't exactly give you confidence.

Although no record was kept, the colt probably began simple driving lessons around his first birthday. Early instruction consisted of schooling in harness: how to stand still to be hitched, how to move forward even though something seemed to be pulling on you, how not to fuss too much if something pinched or rubbed you.

A horse who trusted people would have been asked within a few days of first being harnessed to accept ground driving. That means his trainer would stand behind him with the reins in his hands asking the young horse, colt, or foal to go forward. It's a less traumatic experience than having to listen to a wheeled vehicle squeak and roll. Most trainers of driving horses do plenty of ground driving before hitching a young horse.

Messner and Wattles were in no hurry with the colt. Today, many of the most important races and the biggest purses are aimed at two-year-old Standardbreds and nearly all healthy young horses with expectations of racing are hitched to training vehicles by the age of eighteen months. In 1897 two-year-old racing was unheard of, so Messner and Wattles probably went slowly with cart work.

Zelica's colt had an uneventful year in 1897. He, being fond of people, was said to have happily accepted his training with little fuss and had no problems worth remembering. There is one surviving story from that year: the legend that Dan Messner attempted to trade the colt to John Wattles for one of Wattles's own yearlings.

It's impossible to know if the story is true. Neither man mentioned it later, but perhaps they couldn't be expected to. Messner would not have wanted to admit that he had been ready to give up on the colt, and Wattles wouldn't have wanted to admit that he had been unwilling to make the trade.

But there may be a ring of truth to the legend. Wattles had been urging Messner to keep faith in the Joe Patchen-Zelica breeding, in spite of the colt's conformation problems. Messner might well have expected Wattles to put his money where his mouth was.

Wattles had probably done no more than ground drive the colt and could not yet judge his speed, especially if Mickey Maguire hadn't shared the story of the colt's mad dash after his mother down the road to Oxford. In spite of what Wattles was telling Messner, there would be no way to know for sure if the colt could race until he was asked for speed in front of a vehicle.

In July 1897 comes the first evidence that Messner expected to race the colt. He applied for an official name with the American Trotting Association, the governing body responsible for harness racing in the Midwest. The Association set race regulations, maintained records, and approved names. Even though betting was illegal in most of the states covered by the Association, the sport's officials wanted to make sure that duplicate names didn't confuse fans.

Dan Messner asked for the name Dan Patchen for his colt, using his own first name, plus Patchen to represent the colt's sire. As an alternative, he suggested Dan P. The requests, particularly Dan, were predictable. Messner had a great deal of emotional investment in the colt, to say nothing of the outlay, and it was natural that the two should share a name. Patchen was also predictable. Each month that went by it became a name of increasing importance in the sport, and any owner of a Joe Patchen foal wanted people to know it.

Neither name was available. On July 20, 1897, Messner received word from the Trotting Association that his Joe Patchen-Zelica colt had been given the official name of Dan Patch.

Dan for him and Patch instead of Patchen—not quite what he wanted, but not bad. Dan Messner was pleased.

Years later, some people—not people in Oxford, to be sure—came to believe that Dan Patch had been named for Sam Patch. A human celebrity of the early nineteenth century, Sam Patch leaped from ships, across gorges, and down waterfalls—wherever he could find a crowd. But Dan Patch was named for his family, equine and human.

Regardless of its source, Zelica's colt now had a real name. To be honest, people in Oxford had already stopped calling him Messner's Folly. Not that his legs had suddenly become correct or anything, but this shiny-coated colt with the intelligent eyes no longer looked like such a mistake.

The year 1897 was also important to Dan Patch for what didn't happen to him. He was not gelded. Although it was a little less common a hundred years ago, owners routinely had their male yearlings neutered unless they expected them to have value as breeding animals.

Experts have never entirely agreed on whether stallions or geldings make better racing and working horses, with some people arguing that stallions have greater fire and determination while geldings are better able to concentrate on their work and are much easier to handle.

By 1897 the balance of opinion had begun to lean towards gelding workhorses or a racehorse of limited promise, while leaving a good racing prospect intact. Messner's decision against gelding Dan Patch may have been a consequence of the colt's good breeding, plus his easygoing nature. Or maybe something significant was beginning to show in him.

The first stories of Dan Patch pulling a cart date from early 1898. Residents of Oxford, as well as people living along the road to the Wattles farm, began to take note of the seventy-one-year-old John Wattles and the two-year-old Dan Patch. The men looked closely at the colt, gathering information for livery stable discussions about whether or not Dan Messner might have a race-horse after all. The children were more interested in the sight of the very old man and the very young horse, the man's long white beard flowing in the wind just like colt's black mane and tail.

The tax assessor for Benton County looked closely enough to rate Dan Patch at $200 in July, an unusually high amount for an unraced colt who, so the experts said, still had leg problems. John Wattles's filly Joan Patchen had been assessed for one hundred dollars, even though those same experts said she was absolutely correct in her conformation.

In reality, Dan Patch was growing out of his problems. He was still short-bodied and long-legged and always would be. To eyes used to spotting good trotter conformation, such a body shape could look awkward and ungraceful. He did have the classic trotting pitch, with his hindquarters higher than his withers, but that build might be a little suspect in a horse destined to be a pacer. But in spite of the physical contradictions, he was a handsome colt.

His knees did remain a little prominent. People who watched John Wattles drive him at an increasingly rapid speed on the roads outside Oxford came to agree that the big knees appeared not to matter. Although the knees of a racing pacer have to be flexible, they don't have to flex as much as a trotter's. At a fast trot, a horse's legs bend so much that the hoof almost touches the elbow where the leg connects to the body. The pacer's knee doesn't have to fold nearly so much and big knees, if otherwise sound, aren't a major problem for a pacing horse.

The biggest problem for any racing harness horse is interference, when one hoof touches another hoof or, even worse, another part of his body. A short-bodied trotter is almost guaranteed to interfere with himself, since the hindleg on one side of the body moves forward as the foreleg on the same side moves back. Without good body length, that back hoof is going to hit somewhere on the foreleg. It happens in all breeds and is known by the general term "forging" if the rear hoof strikes the front one. It's often corrected by using lighter shoes in front, allowing a quicker takeoff.

You also don't want your trotter to be too long in the leg, for the same reason. Even if the length of the body is adequate, long legs are more likely to interfere with each other. But a short-bodied, long-legged horse has a perfectly fine conformation if he happens to pace.

A pacer, whose legs on each side of the body move forward and back in unison, can't interfere with the leg on the same side and can't, strictly speaking, forge. He can interfere with legs on opposite sides, though. The most common pacing interference is cross-firing, when a rear hoof clips the front hoof on the other side of the body. Narrow-bodied horses can cross-fire, as can horses whose rear ankles and hooves don't travel straight.

Dan Patch, as he grew from a yearling to a two-year-old, had widened in the body, particularly the chest. People who appreciated pacers grew in their admiration of how he was put together. Those long legs promised a long racing stride, maybe like Joe

Patchen's monster twenty-three-foot step. There was still the problem of the left hind leg that flared a little. Funny thing, though. In motion in front of a vehicle, Dan Patch's left hind didn't look quite so bad anymore and the rest of his legs were beginning to look just about right.

But Wattles and Messner had a closeup look. As Dan Patch was asked for speed, he did tend to cross-fire. They knew his gait needed work.

There is no really good Standardbred racehorse who doesn't have a good gait, and most horses become a little better-gaited with skilled shoeing. Messner and Wattles tried several blacksmiths and eventually came up with a system that worked. They chose light five ounce shoes, with a little extra section on the back of the left rear, called a trailer, designed to provide a larger base for stability. More important, the trailer slowed down the leg just enough to prevent the cross-firing and smooth out the gait. The light shoes in front also helped the opposite front hoof get out of the way.

Dan Patch, the crooked-legged foal who couldn't stand to nurse was now, two years later, a pacer of fine conformation and decent gait. Years later Messner said Harry Haws, the Pennsylvania businessman who had been the underbidder on Zelica three years earlier, offered $1,000 for the still unraced Dan Patch. Messner was pleased but not tempted. This story suggests that Zelica had been a special prize all along, if a rich Easterner had kept such a close eye on her offspring.

The offer, event though it wasn't accepted, was enough to prompt the first ever example of Dan Patch's name being used to promote a product or service. At the end of the summer, Taylor's

Blacksmith, one of the shops that had worked on the shoeing problem, advertised themselves as Dan Patch's farrier, hoping to compete favorably with Oxford blacksmith Elisha Johnson. He advertised himself as a "scientific shoer."

Dan Patch's working life was still more fun than labor, for both him and his owner. Zelica was sometimes still used as a buggy horse, but she was back in foal, and Dan Messner saw no reason not to use her son in front of his runabout. The admiring looks he used to get while driving Zelica were multiplied when he drove the colt. Everybody in Oxford had heard about that thousand-dollar offer.

Messner believed that working Dan Patch at buggy speed would help in his preparation for racing, and this idea wasn't considered foolish, in spite of the colt's value. Even today, a promising young Standardbred might be driven casually, even by an amateur, although none would be risked on a public road.

Certainly none would be asked to do what Dan Patch did over the winter of 1898-1899. Once the snow came, Messner traded his buggy for a sleigh. The small boys of Oxford were welcome to grab onto the back of the cutter and be pulled on their sleds by a colt worth a thousand dollars. It was, they said, like flying.

Years later, Dan Messner claimed that it was during these daily outings with both the buggy and the sleigh that he had his first fleeting thought that Dan Patch might turn out to be more than just a quick, well-bred horse. Messner discovered that Dan Patch, who looked so big, lazy, and cheerful, loved to go fast, reveling in speed for its own sake. There was more. When another horse came alongside, Dan Patch would not permit him to pass. He simply wouldn't allow it, no matter what the two drivers wanted. Whether he was asked to go fast or not, Dan Patch would stretch those long legs, lower his head, banish the amiable look from his face, and fly.

In nature, horses are more cooperative than competitive. They are herd animals and the desire to be together is a profound and essential part of their natures. Stallions will compete over mares, and all horses will compete over food if the supply is limited, either in reality or in their imaginations. But most domesticated horses older than six months have little interest in proving who's best. Those who are interested tend to be smart, older, and highly experienced. They also tend to be very good at the careers chosen for them.

The fact that Dan Patch was so competitive as an inexperienced two-year-old had people in Oxford shaking their heads. What might happen, they wondered, when he actually set foot on a racetrack?

5

A RACEHORSE AFTER ALL

THERE IS NO sensation more acute than the anticipation felt by people connected to an unraced young horse. After his first race, you pretty much know what you have, but until then your horse can be anything. He can be the fastest horse ever to set foot on a racetrack. Never mind that he's not so quick in his training; you can believe that he's so brave and determined that the mere presence of competition will make him fly. So you spend a lot of time imagining the riches and the fame and the joy he might bring you.

But there's pain as well as pleasure in that anticipation. If you even slightly know horses, you realize they can get sick or hurt without the faintest warning. You also know that the most promising young horses in the world sometimes are inexplicably slow on the track, nervous, scared, cowardly, or something else that makes them losers rather than winners.

Dan Messner and John Wattles experienced the highs and lows of anticipation during 1898 and 1899. They suspected they might have something special, and dared to hope, but they knew that the majority of promising young horses become increasingly less promising as they approach their racing careers.

Sometimes it's age alone that dims the talent that burns so brightly in a young animal. The height and weight that come with age may change a horse's balance and center of gravity just enough to take away his speed. Sometimes the horse simply doesn't stay sound under the stress of training. His legs or feet or body start to hurt and he can't move as fast as he did as a fresh young animal.

Messner and Wattles must have worried, in those last months before racing, that Dan Patch might be in that second category. He was the son of the Iron Horse, true, but he was also the son of the sore-legged Zelica, who was sound enough to pull a buggy and carry babies, but not sound enough to race.

There are milestones to pass in those final months, and for some horses the milestones become mountains that can't be climbed. For Dan Patch, there were two important steps that could have derailed the whole trip, had the wrong choices been made.

John Wattles began training Dan Patch on a real, honest-to-goodness racetrack late in the summer of 1898 or, more likely, in the spring of 1899. The half-mile track was in Templeton, a few miles east of Oxford.

Colonel William Templeton, a son of early Indiana land seekers who made a great deal of money in cattle, decided to put some of that money into a racing surface for the first Benton County Fair in 1871. Templeton, who earned his rank in the

DAN PATCH'S FIRST RACE TRACK

A postcard from about 1905 shows the Chiquesalonghi racetrack just a few years after Dan Patch learned his early racing lessons there.

Civil War, had sold his farm to Patrick Kennedy but the track remained.

Kennedy, although his Irish ancestors loved running horses, preferred trotters himself and maintained the racing surface in good condition. He also retained the name Colonel Templeton had given to his track: Chiquesalonghi, said to be the word for "beautiful spot" in the language of the Miami, or maybe the Shawnee. It appears not to have come from the local Potawatomi, whose language rarely included the letter "l."

No one remembered from experience where the name came from, but the definition seemed appropriate. The track stood on some of the finest farmland in western Indiana. Dan Patch was one of dozens of young horses who trained seriously over the Templeton track during the last years of the nineteenth century.

The first time on a real racetrack is a milestone in a racehorse's life. He will experience other horses doing the same thing he is and he will do it in front of people watching and making noise. Because of all the talk around Oxford about Dan Messner's quick colt, every time Dan Patch paced onto the Templeton track he had an audience.

The young Dan Patch reveled in the racetrack atmosphere. He loved attention and welcomed the pats and pokes of young boys. He also enjoyed the attention of men who had heard talk of the fast colt from Oxford and were convinced that they had a faster one.

One of those men was Benjamin T. Lee, a landowner from the eastern part of Benton County. Lee had the money and time to indulge in horse racing and had acquired a small bay pacing colt from Kentucky. The colt was fast and brave and Lee was convinced that his colt could stay with Dan Messner's.

He could, but only for a quarter mile or so. Dan Patch, once he got his long legs arranged and his gait organized, pulled away from any horse who dared to challenge him, requiring little or no encouragement from Wattles. Several times Lee drove his little bay at racing speed against Dan Patch, but each time the result was the same. The Kentucky colt was left in the dust of the Chiquesalonghi track.

It was clear that Dan Patch loved the idea of racing—the competition, the challenge, the physical and mental pleasure of it. He especially loved racing in front of a crowd. Dan Messner and John Wattles were almost convinced that they had a real racehorse on their hands.

Almost, because Dan Patch still had a problem that hadn't quite been solved by the special shoeing. The sickly foal who couldn't stand to nurse had grown into a big horse, close to his full adult height and weight as a three-year-old. A few years later, he stood sixteen hands and weighed nearly 1200 pounds. Even today, that would make him a big Standardbred. At three he was only a little under that height.

He was not just tall but was now wide in the hindquarters. The misshapen left hind hoof paddled even wider at high speeds, causing him to strike the left wheel of John Wattles' training cart. Wattles decided that his old cart wouldn't do and a new, wider one would have to be made.

An Oxford blacksmith, possibly Mr. Taylor although the story isn't complete, made a heavy oak jog cart with extra wide wheels. With the custom-made cart, Dan Patch no longer interfered with the wheel. The blacksmith was engaged to make a racing sulky too, although Wattles and Messner were determined not to race the colt until he was a full-grown four-year-old.

Messner and Wattles were hardly alone in their efforts to find the ideal vehicle. Blacksmiths, carriage makers, and tinkerers were putting together special sulkies and carts in sheds and shops across the Midwest in 1899. The years proceeding Dan Patch's foaling had seen an upheaval in the shape and appearance of racing vehicles.

Several late nineteenth-century developments came together in a lucky confluence to create vehicles that took full advantage of a long-legged, long-striding, fast horse. Dan Patch was going to be a good race horse anyway, but the new sulky design contributed to making him great.

Today, we use the word "sulky" to describe a vehicle pulled by harness racehorses (or a personality trait of somebody who pouts a lot) but until the turn of the nineteenth to the twentieth century the word had a broader meaning. A sulky was a small, single-axle, one-person, horse-drawn vehicle, usually with wheels for the road but sometimes with runners for snow where it would be called a "sulky sleigh."

The word sulky had been used for centuries for single-person vehicles, and some historians believe that the other definition of the word, to describe a glum or mopy person, had the same origin since you aren't very sociable if you want to drive alone. Sulkies were high-wheeled, light, basic, and not very comfortable for the driver, but they were maneuverable in bad conditions and persisted in road use until buggies took over the single-axle business, offering greater comfort for a single driver as well as the ability to carry one or more additional passengers.

Sulkies remained alive and well on the racetrack, where comfort doesn't matter while weight and maneuverability do. With no commercial market beyond the racetrack, sulky designers could concentrate on making their vehicles even lighter and more mobile.

When bicycles began appearing on American streets and sidewalks in the 1880s sulky designers saw the answer to their prayers. After a short flirtation with high-wheel velocipedes, bicycle makers began installing small wheels with pneumatic tires on their contraptions. Their machines now amazed everybody with their speed, agility, and safety.

If bicycles would work so well with little rubber-covered, air-filled wheels, the sulky men said, so could sulkies. It took a few years to convince everyone, but by the time Dan Patch began training at Chiquesalonghi, few of the old high-wheeled sulkies remained in serious use. Some veteran horsemen liked to believe that the high wheels, some as high as five feet, were faster than the small bicycle wheels, but the stopwatch proved otherwise.

At the same time the sulky's wheels were shrinking, its axle was bending. Traditionally, the sulky axle was a straight bar of iron with wheels on either end, with the seat perched between them. But the faster, longer gait of the Hambletonian pacers and trotters was beginning to cause terrible interference with

PACING IN THE LATEST STYLE.

The low-wheeled, low-seated sulky had taken over the sport by the time Dan Patch began his training. *(Lithograph: Currier and Ives)*

this straight bar, especially on the tight turns of half-mile tracks. Trainers tried all kinds of remedies, including long shafts, to hitch the horse well ahead of the axle.

In the late 1870s sulky builders came out with axles that bent in the middle into an upside down U, taking them out of range of the hocks of the fast horses. When, in 1892, the bent axle was combined with bicycle tires, the modern sulky appeared. Other adjustments were made over the next decade and eventually the driver found himself down, out of the air and closer to the horse's hindquarters. The aerodynamics were greatly improved.

Dan Messner was a modern man. He was apparently not modern enough to have a photograph made of his unraced horse in front of a sulky or training cart, but it's reasonable to assume that he wouldn't have permitted an old-fashioned vehicle to be used with his beloved colt. Dan Patch's blacksmith-made training cart, as well as the planned sulky, would have had the modern small wheels and bent axle.

Messner must have had to resist the advice of the men who watched the horses train at Pat Kennedy's track. They probably urged him to give Dan Patch his first race in the summer of 1899, as soon as the problems with cart and sulky were worked out. It was a new world, he must have been told, one where you acted quickly if you wanted to accomplish anything.

Great trotting champions like Lady Suffolk, who made her first official start at the age of five in 1838, and Flora Temple, who first raced as a five-year-old in 1850, may not have competed as three-year-olds. But Standardbreds were bigger now—and none much bigger than Dan Patch. He was already training at racing speed, so the Benton County conventional wisdom said, why not earn a little money and make a little reputation on a real race-track?

Early racing wasn't yet entirely accepted by horsemen in 1899, but even traditionalists like John Wattles did sometimes race young horses. He remembered that his trotting colt Cotton-wood competed at three in 1892, winning several races and a considerable reputation at local fairs as well as earning a hefty price tag at the end of the season.

But maybe it was because of his experience with Cottonwood that Wattles was not among those urging Messner to hurry Dan Patch to the racetrack. Cottonwood, in the hands of his new owner, never amounted to much after his successful three-year-old season. As much as John Wattles might like to think that it was his training that made the difference, he suspected that three-year-old legs and lungs might not always be ready for racing.

Today, no owner or trainer of a healthy young Standardbred would wait until his horse is four. Few even wait until he's three, since purses are so big for two-year-olds. But at the turn of the last century, with less money and fame to be had in individual races, a lucrative career was a long steady one, not a short brilliant one.

So the 1899 summer fair season came and went with Dan Patch still a racehorse-to-be. The two Dans spent the winter of 1899–1900 as they had the previous one: being admired as they glided through the snowy streets of Oxford, allowing young boys to hitch a ride from behind on their sleds. The young Dan Patch was remembered for decades for the free rides he gave, for as long as those young boys lived.

Training resumed with increased intensity in the spring of 1900. Messner and Wattles decided to wait until their local Benton-Warren County fair to give Dan Patch his first start. It was going to be a long wait, since the fair took place the last week of August.

Around the beginning of August, with the horse as fit as he was likely to get, Wattles announced to Messner that it was time to see just how fast Dan Patch could go. Wattles said it was to be a training mile, not a time trial. The colt would pull the heavy oak training cart, not the light new sulky, and he would be timed by stopwatch.

The time for the mile might not be particularly impressive, Wattles warned, not only because of the heavy cart but because they wouldn't be using time trial prompters—other horses to challenge their colt in relays to wring the last second of speed out of him. What's more, although Pat Kennedy maintained the track at Chiquesalonghi as well he was able, it could never produce the kind of speed that an active racetrack would. Still, Wattles would urge Dan Patch to go as fast as he could and the timed mile should give them an idea about what the colt could do and what kind of race he should be entered in.

Because neither Wattles nor Messner expected much from the timed mile, there were only a few spectators at the Templeton track for Dan Patch's appearance. Messner invited his friend Charley Shipps to observe, knowing that Shipps would enjoy watching the colt's newly beautiful gait and hoping that his friend might also see an impressive time, never mind Wattles's warnings. Shipps owned the best furniture store in Oxford but was better known as the operator of a livery stable that specialized in hearses and funeral equipment. To further that business, he had learned to be an embalmer himself. Messner admired Shipps as a man of many talents.

Nobody was prepared for just how impressive Dan Patch turned out to be. After a leisurely warm up, Wattles urged the colt into his full racing pace. Three stopwatches clicked—even Wattles carried one as he drove. The colt sped through the first lap of the half-mile track, his stride as long and smooth as it had ever been.

Wattles, in the cart, and Messner, standing transfixed at track-side, thought at first that the timed mile might not be turning out as well as they hoped. The colt was too smooth, and the strides too easy. He didn't seem to be working hard enough to be fast.

Messner may have glanced at his watch after the first circuit of the half-mile track. Neither of the two men watching the trial bothered to note the interim time, and Wattles was probably too busy to look. He did, however, urge Dan Patch to greater speed.

It was during the final trip around the Templeton track that Messner knew and Wattles suspected that their colt was doing something beyond their most cherished dreams. He was flying. There was no other word to describe it. As Dan Patch swept past the starting point, both men forgot to click their stopwatches. They were too thrilled to remember.

Charley Shipps, although excited too, had the presence of mind to stop his watch. He looked at it, looked again, and told Dan Messner what it said. When Wattles brought Dan Patch back to where they were standing, he could tell from the looks on their faces that the time was good. He couldn't begin to guess how good it was.

Charley Shipps's watch said 2:14—two minutes and fourteen seconds for the mile. That was pulling a heavy, oversized oak training cart, without competition, on a half-mile track, and hand-timed by an amateur (possibly adding as much as a full second to the real time). Just twenty years earlier, that would have been the world record for a pacing mile.

By 1900, the record was much faster. Star Pointer's was 1:59¼, but even Star Pointer's fans might have been happy with a 2:14 mile under the conditions of Dan Patch's training mile. Wattles, Messner, and Shipp argued over just how fast the colt could have gone with a bicycle-wheeled sulky on a real racetrack.

Take off a couple of seconds for the track—most records were set on meticulously maintained mile tracks—and take off another couple for the lack of competition. Take off a second for the stopwatch and another for the heavy training cart, and you're down to 2:08. Don't tell John Wattles, Messner might have said to himself, but take off at least a second for a more accomplished driver and you're down below 2:07. That would have been a world record as recently as 1884. Dan Patch was ready to race—no doubt about that.

Although the colt had trained in front of crowds before, Wattles advised one final appearance as an unraced horse. Messner offered an exhibition race between Dan Patch and any other horse who showed up on August 18, and hundreds of people—mostly from Oxford, but also from Boswell, Templeton, and the other towns in the area—made plans to bring picnic lunches and make a day of it.

Unfortunately for horse and man, a heavy rain on the eighteenth cancelled the exhibition. The spectators instead made plans to see the locally famous young horse in his first real race, scheduled for two weeks later in Boswell.

Most of the 2,000 people of Oxford had planned to go to the Benton-Warren County Agricultural Fair anyway, since it was always the social event of the year, an exclamation point at the end of the summer season. The last five days of August were set aside for fair-going, and only the desperately poor or the utterly unsociable would dream of missing it.

After studying the conditions for the eleven races scheduled for the last couple of days of the fair in Boswell, Wattles and Messner settled on a 2:35 pace. That race was designed for horses who had no official race record below the next fastest category, in this case probably 2:20 for the mile. The faster the level, the higher the purse, so it was a challenge to pick just the right spot to maximize both potential profit and likely success.

They determined between them to tell as few people as possible about the time trial. After all, it didn't really count. Just about everybody in Oxford knew about it, but they and their friends still hoped to get a few lucrative side bets with residents of other towns.

A 2:35 race was, at least to anybody who didn't know about Dan Patch, an ambitious spot for a young horse to start his career. A rival could have previously raced as fast as 2:21 and still qualify. Because races consisted of heats, at least three and possibly four, the inexperienced Dan Patch might have to race four full race miles in one day against proven horses, quite a challenge for a young horse in his first real racing competition. Wattles and Messner were sure he was up to it. Pretty sure, anyway.

Wattles was certainly experienced enough to know, and Messner had seen enough racing to suspect, that some horses who ought to be great aren't even good in a real race. They may be fast, they may be smooth gaited, and they may train well in the company of other horses in front of spectators. But something happens when the race is for real. They race poorly and always do and nobody quite knows why.

Most of the residents of Oxford had no doubts at all. According to the *Oxford Tribune* the next week, every store in town closed so that the people of Dan Patch's home town could see him race. Postmaster James Pickering, although not at all happy about it, was required to stay behind to keep the post office open. He had no business to keep him occupied and spent the afternoon waiting for word from Boswell.

A few of the farmers in the Oxford area chose not to go to the fair on the thirtieth. They were still bringing in their hay and corn and believed they shouldn't miss a day just to see a horse. Many regretted it later, since the race was the only time Dan Patch was ever to race in Benton County. Hay came in year after year, but Dan Patch was, some suspected even then, a horse of a lifetime.

Attendance for that Thursday surprised and pleased the fair organizers. Stunned may have been a better word, since more than 8,000 people paid their fifty cents to get in. Some of the officials had no idea why so many people had showed up for the fourth day of the fair, certainly never suspecting that the 2:35 pace might be the big attraction.

It had been a hot, dry summer, and August 30 brought more of the same. Good news for the 8,000 fans who weren't going to have to seek shelter out of view of the racing, and good news for anybody who wanted a race that would really show what Dan Patch could do. The remaining skeptics, mostly residents of Boswell and Warren, were pleased too. There would be no excuses for the young horse that everybody was talking about.

The hot sun meant something more to the horsemen among the 8,000. For some reason not known then and still not entirely understood, even in these days of blood analysis and endoscopic examination of lungs, harness race horses go faster in hot clear weather. It doesn't make a lot of sense, since horses as a species tend to thrive in the cold, but most records are set on hot, even scorching, days. If Dan Messner's young horse was as good as the Oxford people believed, the race times should show it.

As at other fair racing events in Indiana, betting was illegal at the Benton-Warren County Fair, so we have no idea whether Dan Patch was favored in his first start. Oxford people were probably able to get some private bets on the hometown colt, although only two other horses were entered in the 2:35 pace.

The race, when it came late in the afternoon, was an anticlimax. John Wattles, wearing a blue cap and gold-trimmed jacket, merely urged the colt into a pace and Dan Patch took it from there. Decades later, the people who remembered seeing the race (and almost every resident of Oxford later claimed they did) largely recalled the sight of Wattle's long beard flowing behind his head as the young horse sped around the track.

Three heats and three easy wins later, Messner's Folly had won a real race. There was bedlam in the stands, with the fans screaming and roaring at the sight they had seen.

The times, although much better than the 2:35 standard of the race, were good but not spectacular: 2:24½, 2:22¼, and 2:24½. Why hadn't the hot day and competition, modest as it was, led to faster times? Probably because Wattles and Messner hadn't wanted them. After a comfortable and safe win in his first start, Dan Patch remained eligible for future 2:35 races.

Possibly more to the point, Dan Patch still had a few doubters, although not many in Oxford. There would be side bets to be had later in the fall racing season at other fairs in Indiana. The race featured a $250 purse, with half of that—$125—going to the winner with the losers, Prince Medium and Merrygo, dividing up the rest. In one afternoon, Dan Patch had won for his owner nearly half of the purchase price of his mother.

By August 30, Dan Messner had already discovered that owning a good race horse could be lucrative. He had been offered, and turned down, $1,000 for the colt. After the race, he realized that owning a good horse with a compelling personality could be very lucrative indeed. Although he still loved his young horse as he had before, his attitude toward Dan Patch now underwent a subtle change.

That night, residents of Oxford pulled out some leftover Fourth of July fireworks and conducted an impromptu celebration in the town square, shooting off roman candles and firecrackers. Dan Messner and John Wattles watched the merriment for a few minutes before going home, Wattles to check on the subject of the celebration and Messner to compose the weekly ad for his store.

The following week's *Oxford Tribune,* which featured the story of the Boswell Fair race on the first page, included the weekly Messner and Son store ad on the last page where Oxford's new hero appeared again: "Dan Patch in the Lead," the ad began in huge letters. "We are again IN THE LEAD this fall with the biggest, best, and cheapest line of ladies' silk waists, fall dress goods and trimmings," the ad continued.

The fair racing season was short in Indiana, so Dan Patch was given only five days of rest before traveling to Lafayette, twenty miles away, for that city's bigger and more important fair. It was a much more challenging venue for the horse's second race, an event featuring some of the best horses from the Indiana fair circuit. Some had even enjoyed success in other states. The Lafayette race would offer a $300 purse, enough to attract a big field. Dan Patch was still eligible for the 2:35, in spite of the good times in his first race.

Oxford people remained convinced that Dan Patch would shine even in stellar company, so they descended on Lafayette by the hundreds on Wednesday, September 5, thanks in particular to a discounted round-trip train fare. Most of the Oxford people were convinced that they would see another easy straight-heat win by their colt, but others in the crowd still had doubts. There were plenty of people willing to take the Oxford bets.

Each of the other eight horses was older and more experienced in racing than Dan Patch, and their drivers were also more experienced, although certainly not older, than John Wattles. Exactly what happened in the first heat of that September 5 is still debated, more than a hundred years later.

It was a large field, especially for a fair event, and Wattles drew a second-tier position for his horse. Five or six horses—the stories aren't specific—lined up at the start, with the rest of the field in back of them. While hardly desirable, this isn't a major obstacle, since the first half mile is usually spent settling in. With a careful driver, a good horse can overcome the few-yards head start of the front-tier horses with time to spare.

But published reports describe a rough race, with Dan Patch jostled and squeezed back into a pocket. Not until the field swept around the final turn did Wattles have his horse settled into his perfect pace, and the post that marked the finish came up a few strides too soon. Although spectators described him as flying at the finish, Dan Patch failed to catch Milo S. by a rapidly diminishing head. The time of the race: 2:18½.

It was Dan Patch's first loss, and the Oxford fans were stunned, particularly those who had bet a few dollars on him. Spectators began immediately to debate the cause of the loss.

Bad racing luck, some said. Others blamed John Wattles for making the bad luck, allowing his horse to be trapped behind others and waiting too long to break free. Because of the spectacular finish, few people—even the non-Oxford ones—blamed the horse. He wasn't beaten by a better horse. That much was clear to the people who saw the race.

The fair officials had their own suspicions. After the horses were taken from the track to prepare for the second heat, they called Wattles to the judges' room. Why, they asked him, would an obviously superior horse take so long to get moving? Did his driver hold him back?

No, Wattles said. He was trying a new harness on Dan Patch and unfamiliarity with it slowed both of them down. The judges, still suspicious, told Wattles that a horse whose driver didn't sufficiently try would be disqualified. With that, John Wattles and Dan Patch went off to win three straight heats by big margins, the fastest in 2:16.

The story went around that Wattles did indeed hold his horse and intended to either prevent his winning the first heat or to make his win look unimpressive. Apparently, the motive was that he and his friends would be able to find more willing bets on the second heat. But it's also possible that Wattles, knowing that one heat doesn't make a race, decided that asking the young horse for the extra effort needed to overcome the poor position would take too much out of him and jeopardize the race.

At any rate, Dan Patch was still unbeaten in his races, if not in heats. His reputation had suffered nothing more than a tiny pinprick.

A week later, on Wednesday, September 12, Messner shipped Dan Patch forty miles to the Montgomery County Fair in Crawfordsville, where he faced eight other horses, including an outstanding pacing mare named American Belle, in another

$300 race. Neither she nor any of the others produced any significant competition, and Dan Patch won the race in straight heats in times of 2:19¾, 2:20¾, and 2:20½. The times were less impressive than he might have managed, but their consistency suggested that they were just what John Wattles wanted.

The Crawfordsville race was followed nine days later by a $400 race in Brazil, sixty miles from Oxford. The tactics were a little different in Brazil, since the race came precisely one week before a much more significant event.

This was a race in Terre Haute, the largest city in western Indiana. The climax of the fair racing season occurred at Terre Haute each September, and the best horses from Indiana and Ohio, as well as a few from the higher level of racing known as the Grand Circuit, took part. What's more, the top drivers, trainers, and owners from throughout the Midwest converged on the city for the week of racing. The track was known to be lightning fast and Wattles and Messner knew that the race would tell them the truth about their mahogany colt.

Wattles, they decided, would ask Dan Patch for a little more effort at the Brazil Fair. They got it. Again, he paced to a straight-heat victory: 2:16¾, 2:19¼, and 2:17¼. Fast—but not as fast as he could go. His earnings for the 1900 season now totaled $625, more than Messner had paid for Zelica, Joe Patchen's stud fee, and some of the boarding expenses for the past four years.

More important, Dan Patch was perfectly set to show his best in Terre Haute. Everybody in Oxford who could get away made plans to travel to the big city on Friday, September 28, and the Chicago and Eastern Illinois Railroad helped. A one dollar round trip excursion train left at 5:40 AM, carrying almost 200 people. Another 300 got on at stops along the eighty-mile route.

But they were destined to be disappointed. Heavy rains that week had left the racetrack too muddy for safe racing, and the racing card was cancelled. The bedraggled group returned to Oxford and the little towns along the way by return train.

With the 1900 fair season over, Messner shipped Dan Patch home with still no proof that his horse could compete at the highest levels of his sport. He suspected Dan Patch belonged at the top, but Messner felt somehow that he and his horse had let the people of Oxford down, even though he had no control over the weather. He had wanted so much to show the world how good his horse really was.

Messner couldn't shake his gloomy feeling as he watched groom Jim Stephen lead Dan Patch down the ramp from the livestock car that had carried him from Terre Haute. Then he noticed that his horse had company. Dozens of Oxford residents had walked, driven, and ridden to the train station to meet the horse they considered their own. Messner's mood brightened considerably as he watched the people of the town walk in front of, alongside, and behind Dan Patch as he was led to the barn behind the Messner house.

It was an impromptu parade, the first to be held in honor of Dan Patch. More than that, it was probably the first real indication of the extraordinary magnetism of Dan Messner's dark brown horse. There may have been handsomer horses in the world and there were, at least to that point, horses with faster racing records. But there was probably no horse anywhere in October 1900 that could prompt a spontaneous escort of dozens of his fellow citizens, just because his big race was rained out.

Dan Messner had always believed that Zelica's crooked-legged colt was special. He now had plenty of proof that he had been right, but even he couldn't have predicted how the colt would touch the imaginations of so many people. It wasn't just admiration of speed and determination or appreciation of equine good looks. It was something akin to love, and Dan Patch's ability to prompt that was very special indeed.

6

ON THE WINGS OF THE WIND

IT WAS A religious era, and Americans at the turn of the last century were fond of finding quotations from the Bible to illustrate and explain nearly everything. The tenth verse of the eighteenth psalm seemed especially appropriate as talk in Oxford turned, as it often did in that winter of 1900–1901, to Dan Patch.

"He did fly upon the wings of the wind," David sang of his God in that beautiful psalm. The same words could be said of Oxford's favorite horse. There couldn't be anything wrong in saying so, since God must surely admire a good horse too.

Some people did believe it was a little sacrilegious when George Gillett, an Oxford cigar maker, began turning out Dan Patch cigars that winter. Gillett used to rent office space above the Messner store and George had remained on good terms with Dan Messner. Naming a cigar for the superlative Dan Patch was a compliment to the human Dan, he believed. It might also sell a few additional cigars for George Gillett

Some people grumbled that an honest purse for a victory was one thing, but profiting from a horse's good name was something else entirely. The cigars were first-rate, though, and cost only a nickel.

Gillett made the Dan Patch cigars more for amusement than profit, and the backbone of his business remained the cigars he manufactured under his company name. He was one of thousands of cigar makers in North America. Cigar smoking was so widespread that most of them could make a good living.

The smelly air that pervaded most public places had led to a female-initiated anti-smoking crusade. It was natural for cigar makers to try to improve the image of their products, if not their odoriferous nature, by using respectable names to advertise them. So Henry Clay cigars sold well in the middle south, and cigars named for Civil War hero Ulysses Grant did well in the North (never mind that Grant died of smoking-induced throat cancer). In the Oxford area, you couldn't find a name much more respectable than Dan Patch.

Dan Messner and his friends undoubtedly smoked a few cigars that winter, whether of the Dan Patch label or not, as they discussed the horse's future. Messner believed that the horse deserved more than a couple years dominating the competition at local fairs for $300 purses and thought he could prove himself one of the best horses in the country if he faced better competition.

Thirty years earlier, he would have had to ship Dan Patch east in search of horses swift enough to tap his still-unknown reserves of speed. Harness racing had developed and prospered along the

Eastern Seaboard, and as late as 1870 trotting tracks hugged the coastline as if they featured wind-filled sails rather than muscle-powered hooves.

The great horses of the mid-nineteenth century were foaled and raced and lived out their lives within a few dozen miles of the shore. From New Jersey's Goldsmith Maid, to Long Island's Lady Suffolk, to Dexter and Hambletonian and Flora Temple from upstate New York—the big names were easterners. They set their records at the Beacon Course in New Jersey and the Fashion Course on Long Island and Suffolk Park in Philadelphia. These and other tracks offered big purses and lured huge crowds.

Owners of fast horses did occasionally venture inland. Flora Temple beat two local horses in Kalamazoo, Michigan in 1859, and Dexter Park in Chicago offered good enough purses to lure Dexter himself to Illinois in 1866. The travel didn't harm the horses and the purses certainly didn't harm their owners' pocketbooks.

In 1871, flush with post–Civil War cash, operators of four non-East Coast racetracks arranged a circuit of races, so that an owner could put a good horse on a train, race him in Springfield, Massachusetts, then put him back on the train to send him to Buffalo, then on to Cleveland and Detroit. A few years later, after other tracks were added to the mix, the organization adopted the name Grand Circuit for their big-money, high-prestige series.

The Grand Circuit races were the fastest and richest in the country. All the member tracks were a full mile around and the fact that you had to go around only two turns, not four, per mile assured the fastest speeds the horses were capable of. The purses seemed huge, at least compared to what was offered at the county fairs.

By the final months of 1900, midwestern horsemen like Dan Messner knew they didn't have to ship a good horse to Long Island or Philadelphia to look for competition. He figured the Grand Circuit would be Dan Patch's stage for fame and riches.

There was one not-so-little problem, though. John Wattles, now nearly seventy-three, may have been the best horseman in Benton County, but even he thought he might have trouble at the Grand Circuit level. He was unfamiliar with the tracks, knew few of the drivers, and had little experience in the long-distance shipping of horses.

What's more, Messner suspected that Dan Patch's gaiting problem, the wide action in back, hadn't entirely been solved. The horses who showed up at Indiana fairs might not be able to exploit the situation, but Grand Circuit horses surely would.

The decision to try the Grand Circuit came quickly and easily, but the choice of a new trainer and driver did not. During the fall of 1900, Messner and friends discussed just about every prominent handler of horses. They even dared to talk about the legendary Budd Doble, who had driven the even more legendary Goldsmith Maid.

Doble certainly knew his way around fast horses. His charges had broken the world record for a mile no fewer than eleven times. But Doble was getting along in years. He was pushing sixty and didn't seem to be quite the right match for the young Dan Patch. They never considered the possibility that the world's most prominent driver and trainer might not be willing to handle an obscure Indiana horse.

Myron McHenry, the "demon of the homestretch." *(Photo: Book and Tables of Sires 1894)*

They talked about Edward Geers, already known as "Pop," even though he wasn't quite fifty. Geers was a man who knew pacers, having set records with such stars as Mattie Hunter and Little Brown Jug, for whom pacing's greatest race was later named. Geers was also a man who knew sulkies, having been almost single-handedly responsible for the rapid and widespread acceptance of the bicycle wheel a decade earlier.

But Geers was known as the "Silent Man" for his calm demeanor and soft voice. He might be steady and smart, but Messner and Wattles thought his quiet nature might be too much of a good thing, given Dan Patch's placid personality. So they settled on forty-four-year-old Myron McHenry.

To Dan Messner, McHenry's nicknames said it all. To harness racing fans at the turn of the last century, McHenry was the "demon of the homestretch." To horsemen, he was "America's greatest reinsman." A horse who flew on the wings of the wind, Messner believed, deserved a man who did the same.

Dan Messner, who went to whatever racetrack he could reach whenever he had a free day, had probably seen Myron McHenry race, but he may not have understood the famous horseman's reputation. McHenry was a volatile, even troubled man, prone to dramatic mood swings and bitter conflicts, sometimes with the people he worked for.

But as difficult as Myron McHenry might sometimes be with people, he was beyond question a man who understood what made a racehorse, and he treated his good ones with extravagant affection. He was, twenty-five years into his racing career, a trainer of outstanding ability and about as skilled a driver of harness race horses as it was possible to be.

Much as Dan Patch did, Myron McHenry represented his time and place to perfection. He, like the horse he would be asked to handle, was a midwesterner, although from Illinois rather than Indiana. They were both products of the relentless move west, the pushing outward of the American frontier.

Myron was the grandson of a traveling Methodist preacher. His father, Daniel McHenry, had settled in Pink Prairie near Geneseo in western Illinois, where he enjoyed great success at farming. Daniel was as pious as his father, but he preferred working the land to spreading the word of God across it. He insisted that his children work hard, refrain from frivolous pursuits, and abstain from alcohol. Somehow his second child Myron developed a taste for alcohol, a distaste for farm work, and an extraordinary fondness for fast horses.

In 1874, Myron reached the age of eighteen and the end of his patience with the slow pace of life on an Illinois farm. His conflict with Daniel escalated through the early part of the year, probably because of Myron's drinking and possibly because of his attraction to horse racing. Late in the spring, Myron left the farm in Pink Prairie for Iowa.

He stopped in Grand Junction, northwest of Des Moines, where he had relatives. He had a change of heart, although not enough to return to the farm in Henry County. In a letter to his sister Lucinda, Myron displayed a serious case of guilt for the manner of his departure from home.

"I hope you all will forgive me for the way I left," he wrote to Lucinda. "I am sorry I done as I did. . . . I am determined to steady down for I know that is the only salvation for me now."

Myron added that he would either work for a carpet layer for fifty cents a day, which he somehow felt was better pay than the fifteen dollars a month he would earn working on an Iowa farm. Perhaps some of the conflict with his father was because he didn't pay proper attention to school.

If Myron ever went to work as a carpet layer he didn't last long. Within weeks he was off to Prairie City, just east of Des Moines, where his uncle Alfred McHenry ran a livery stable and hotel.

If the letters home had given Daniel hope his son had finally placed both feet firmly on the Methodist straight and narrow path, he was to be sadly disappointed. Thanks to Alf McHenry's livery stable, Myron for the first time found himself in direct contact with professional racing men.

Iowa in the 1870s was a paradise for a young man who loved racing. The state had an active fair racing circuit, as well as informal tracks laid out right down the main street of dozens of Iowa towns. The Grandview course in Dubuque was typical. Racing enthusiasts marked off a one-mile distance on a straight road a hundred feet wide, and a full field of trotters could compete at speeds that rivaled times on proper eastern racetracks.

In the summer of 1874, racing driver C. W. Parker hired Myron to take care of his horses for the summer fair circuit. In letters to Lucinda, Myron describes visits to Ottumwa and Oskaloosa, to Keokuk and Albia, to Indianola and Eddyville. Life on a racing circuit, Myron discovered, was nothing like a once-a-year visit to a county fair.

Myron also discovered that he was good at taking care of racehorses, good enough that Parker offered him a job as a groom for the horses during the winter off season. The time with Parker taught Myron McHenry about training and probably gave him a chance to drive during training sessions. It's possible he even drove in a few minor races, although there's no record of it.

Myron may have thought he knew a little more than he did, because it appears he lost his job with Parker. By January of 1875, still in Iowa, he was talking about returning to school in the spring so in a few years he could "get a job to make me some money without hard work attached to it." That attitude, as well as a drunken fight at a billiard hall, which he reported to Lucinda, couldn't have helped his standing at home.

As far as we know, Myron McHenry never went back to school. He continued grooming racehorses and, in 1877, was hired by D. C. Gifford of Prairie City to train a horse named Grapevine on the summer Iowa fair circuit.

At the end of the 1878 racing season, twenty-two-year-old Myron was back in Henry County, where he married eighteen-year-old Ida Gierhart of Atkinson. They may have met through Methodist church circles. Her father, Christian, was a pillar of the church in Geneseo, having been Sunday school superintendent for many years. Assuming that Myron had been a student there, Christian might well have had fears for the success of his daughter's marriage—fears that turned out to be well founded.

Myron tried to make a life away from racing, possibly because his new wife and her parents joined his own family in urging him to do so. He got a job in a livery stable in Geneseo, but liveries in Illinois weren't much different from those in Indiana and Iowa. Talk of racing was everywhere, and sometimes the racehorses were there too.

On July 4, 1880, Myron McHenry drove his first official race, four times around the central square in Galva, a few miles from Geneseo. He won, with a trotting mare named Princess, and there was now no chance he would do anything else for a living. Over the next few years, he became locally famous, winning dozens of races at county fairs.

As Dan Messner was going to realize years later, local fame tends not to be enough when you have great faith in your own abilities, and Myron McHenry moved on to the Grand Circuit in 1886, just after his thirtieth birthday. He was hired as a trainer and driver by Thomas Applebee, a former resident of Geneseo who campaigned a string of trotters.

Myron McHenry's fame spread with the success of Mabel A. She was a hard-to-handle trotting mare from whom he coaxed a 2:23¼ mile, an outstanding time for a young mare pulling a high-wheeled sulky. By the end of the 1886 Grand Circuit season, McHenry was known around the country as a good trainer and an even better driver, one who could, almost by sheer will, get spectacular times from less-than-spectacular horses.

McHenry was something the sport had been waiting for: a driver just about as good as Budd Doble who had the personality to excite the public imagination. He wasn't uniformly popular with the men he raced against, given his rough style of racing and his even rougher tongue away from the track. But nobody denied his talent.

"He has wonderful hands, steady nerves, and is full of magnetism," one racing writer noted. Another called him the "wizard of the sulky."

For the next fifteen years, McHenry trained and drove one outstanding horse after another on tracks from Boston to Atlanta to San Francisco. He kept in contact with the family in Pink Prairie, training his horses during the off-season on a track he built on McHenry acreage.

He bred a few horses, including a crooked-legged filly named Rose Croix, whom he trained and then drove to victory in the Kentucky Futurity, one of the sport's most important races. More than a hundred years later, Myron McHenry remains the only man to have bred, owned, trained, and driven the same horse to victory in that race.

Everybody heard about that accomplishment, thanks to the burgeoning racing press, but horsemen focused on the fact that he made a winner out of a horse with poor conformation and a bad gait. They also noted that he was especially good with the newly popular pacers, as a native midwesterner should be. He came within half a heartbeat of a two-minute mile with John R. Gentry, the closest any horse had ever come to that milestone.

Daniel McHenry refused to see his son race, in spite of the fact that many of Myron's appearances took place on tracks within an easy train trip of Pink Prairie. Finally, a special occasion lured the devout Methodist to the racetrack: the Chicago World's

Fair. In 1893, thirteen years after Myron began driving in races, Daniel McHenry saw his son perform for the first time. We can be reasonably confident that Daniel didn't place any bets.

Around the same time, Myron moved his off-season training operation to Freeport, Illinois, about a hundred miles away, then moved on to Cleveland a few years later. In the last years of the century, he drove for millionaire James Butler of New York, the creator of the modern supermarket, but that job was now gone.

Dan Patch in May 1901, the day he left Oxford, Indiana, for Cleveland.
(Photo: International Stock Food Farm Yearbook 1906)

Late in 1900 Myron McHenry let the racing world know that he was on the lookout for horses to train and drive, if they were good enough.

Dan Messner was convinced he had one that was. Messner wrote to McHenry, describing Dan Patch's success in his brief racing career, explaining his breeding, and asking if the famous driver was willing to take on the horse for the Grand Circuit.

Myron McHenry showed the letter to a friend, commenting that every owner of a pretty good fair racer thought he had a Grand Circuit horse. But there was something about the pedigree that caught his eye. He'd raced against Joe Patchen and admired the Iron Horse's toughness and determination. There may also have been something about Dan Patch's small-town background that reverberated.

McHenry wrote Messner that the Grand Circuit required money, lots of it, for training and travel. Moreover, even the best training in the world couldn't make an untalented horse competitive at that level of racing. Messner wrote back that he had money, lots of it, and was confident enough in Dan Patch's talent to spend as much as necessary to give him a chance.

Myron McHenry replied that he would consider the horse. He told Messner to ship Dan Patch to Cleveland, suggesting that he would drive some test miles before making a final decision. In reality, he had already decided. In early April 1901 he told a reporter from the *Boston Globe* that Dan Patch would be the first of a select string of four horses that he would train for the upcoming Grand Circuit season. In late April he told a Syracuse newspaper that Dan Patch had extreme speed and was currently managed by his owner, an "aged but inexperienced

Indiana man." There's no record of Messner's reaction to this description.

Dan Patch left Oxford on May 13, 1901. The trip, the longest that Dan Patch had ever made, was accomplished without incident. Dan Messner traveled along so that he could be on hand for the trial, hoping to make the first payment for training expenses. The test, which consisted of several miles around Cleveland's beautiful Glenville racetrack, left Myron McHenry puzzled. The Indiana horse didn't appear to work very hard, wasn't winded, and was utterly unexcited by the unfamiliar racetrack.

His first thought was that Dan Patch had none of the competitive spark, to say nothing of the speed, required for Grand Circuit success. Then he looked at his stopwatch. The horse who seemed to be going so slowly had been flying. After the trial, McHenry hopped off the training cart and walked around the apparently apathetic horse.

Messner later told friends that McHenry spoke directly to the horse after the trial. Nice to know that Oxford people weren't the only ones inclined to give Dan Patch credit for almost human intelligence, he thought.

"You're either the world's biggest counterfeit," McHenry supposedly said, "or you're the fastest horse in the world." Presumably the horse was not insulted, although Messner may have been taken aback by McHenry's bluntness. But McHenry agreed to take on the horse and Dan Messner went home happy, although somewhat poorer.

McHenry had two months before the beginning of the Grand Circuit season. He didn't much like to admit it, but the small town people had done a pretty good job conditioning the now five-year-old horse. He observed that Dan Patch wasn't far short of racing shape, a surprise to him given the length and severity of the midwestern winter. It's unlikely that he knew about Dan Messner's habit of driving his promising young horse to a sleigh.

But he did know that the gaiting problem, the wide action in back, had to be fixed. The local corrective shoeing had helped a little, and McHenry certainly wouldn't have any trouble finding a wide sulky, but neither aid was quite enough for the Grand Circuit.

He had the blacksmith trim each hoof very short at the toe, then nail on a shoe with an unusually high heel in back. Later, observers would say that Dan's hooves looked like the feet of fashionable ladies wearing high French heels, but McHenry didn't care how they looked. He was confident that Dan Patch's hind feet wouldn't interfere with either his front feet or the sulky as he reached Grand Circuit speed.

People who watched the training miles in Cleveland in May and June noted that Myron McHenry had given Dan Patch a gait that wasn't simply correct and beautiful. It was just about perfect, and a glorious thing to see.

7

A STAR IS BORN

IN THE LATE spring of 1901 Myron McHenry faced a dilemma. He greatly enjoyed publicity and included newspapermen among his circle of friends, but he equally enjoyed having the upper hand with bookmakers. As all trainers did— still do, for that matter—he relished getting a hot prospect to the racetrack before anybody else took notice. That meant juicy odds on a horse that was better than people realized. But he found it difficult to keep a secret of Dan Patch, and his own comments didn't help.

The Glenville track was a springtime Mecca for racing men. At the time of Dan Patch's arrival it was thirty years old but still elegant, part of an eighty-seven-acre lakeside park built by Cleveland's wealthy lovers of fine light harness horses. Among its present owners was shipbuilder Harold M. Hanna, brother of Senator Mark Hanna. The two Hannas had parlayed an inherited wholesale grocery business into a massive operation that dominated the shipping of iron ore on the Great Lakes. There was plenty of Hanna money to buy both racetracks and racehorses, should they want to.

During the spring of 1901, Mark Hanna was involved with his duties in Washington, both in the Senate chamber and in the White House, where he was President William McKinley's most trusted advisor. In May, McKinley embarked on a tour of the West Coast, leaving Mark with a little time on his hands. He liked horses, even if he was more interested in politics, and his brother almost certainly updated him on the news from the hometown track, as he had many times in the past.

Sometimes the news included very big names. The best horses of the second half of the nineteenth century had raced at Glenville, and even the notoriously non-sentimental Myron McHenry must have watched his new trainee work while entertaining fleeting thoughts of the great Goldsmith Maid or the glorious Maud S., who had set a world trotting record at Glenville fifteen years earlier. Harold Hanna may also have watched, perhaps planning to tell his brother about the promising new horse.

McHenry had hoped to train Dan Patch in private for seven weeks, find a tune-up race at a good but lightly attended track, then send him on to the opening of the Grand Circuit in Detroit in mid-July, placing a few bets with unwitting bookmakers along the way. Unfortunately for McHenry's financial prospects, racing people by the dozen began hearing talk about his new horse.

Many, including several of McHenry's journalist friends, found themselves trackside in the mornings, in spite of late evenings at the convivial Roadside Club just outside the grounds of the racetrack. They observed, checked their stopwatches, and left with a story to tell, one that McHenry himself contributed to.

The small town horse was fast, a fact that didn't particularly surprise them, considering that Myron McHenry had agreed to take him on. But what was surprising was that the handsome brown horse could make going fast look so easy. A lightly trained five-year-old should have to work hard to go 2:09½ in front of a training cart, but this Indiana horse could do it without breaking a sweat. As soon as they got home to Chicago, or New York, or Boston, they began spreading the word.

One word they spread was "free-legged." Myron McHenry's prospect was training without hopples, and that was something to talk about. A pacer who races without hopples is a rare and wonderful thing nowadays. It wasn't quite so rare in 1901, but fast horses were increasingly seen in them, just twenty-five years after the first appearance of the equipment on a Midwestern racetrack.

Hopples, today more likely to be spelled hobbles, were first used to discourage all the pacing blood that was creeping into harness racing. Trainers had already figured out that natural pacers could sometimes be converted to the more respectable and more lucrative trot with the use of heavy shoes on the front feet. But the heavy weights in front could just as easily turn a reluctant trotter into a lame horse as into a faster trotter.

Several trainers who wanted their natural pacers to trot began experimenting with contraptions featuring loops made of rope or leather straps dangling down from the harness. The loops, one around the top of each leg and connected diagonally, were designed to prevent a horse from choosing to pace instead of trot. Other trainers tried different designs, but most of them reached the same conclusion: The hopples could keep a horse trotting, but they irritated his skin, tired his legs, and rarely made him a better horse.

Just as hopples were about to be consigned to the trash heap of equine history, an Indiana train conductor named John W. Browning took a hundred dollar bet that he could keep a rough-gaited pacer on stride long enough to do a forty second quarter-mile. Browning wondered if connecting the loops laterally rather than diagonally would work on pacers. With the increasing importance of pacing in the Midwest in the last quarter of the nineteenth century, a lot of other trainers had been looking for ways to improve the gait. They wanted to get the trot out of trotting-bred pacers, but they also hoped to solve one of the biggest problems pacers faced.

In the heat of action, harness racehorses often break stride and increase their speed to a gallop. A horse who does this at the trot can regain the proper gait as soon as he's slowed down a little. It's possible for a good trotter to recover from his mistake and win at least a part of the purse.

Pacers who gallop are usually unable to get back on stride without slowing down to a walk or even a complete stop, so a pacer who breaks stride is usually finished for that race. That fact limited the popularity of pacers, with trainers, owners, and particularly spectators who saw their bets evaporate with the first stride of a gallop.

Browning discovered that the newly rigged hopples solved both problems. Most pacers couldn't trot wearing them, no matter how many crosses of Hambletonian appeared in their pedigrees, and it was almost impossible to break from a pace to a gallop with the device on. When in 1874 his horse John B. won a race at Cambridge City, Indiana, the future of hopples and pacers became inextricably linked.

By the spring of 1901 many pacers wore what were derisively called the Indiana Pants or Indiana Underwear with no embarrassment whatsoever. But Myron McHenry figured that you use the equipment you need, no more and no less, and Dan Patch didn't need hopples.

He was a true pacer, in spite of all that trotting blood, and McHenry had realized instantly that he needed no help in staying on gait. Nor did he break stride, usually a habit of excitable horses. Nobody was likely to call Dan excitable.

So the first time Dan Patch walked onto a racetrack under the control of a big-time driver, he did it with his legs free. There is no known photograph of those first training days under Myron McHenry's control, and there is no record of McHenry's choice of other equipment. Later on he did occasionally use knee boots, held up by suspenders, to protect the thin layer of flesh on the knee from being struck by the opposite hind leg as the horse bends his body around turns. Dan Patch was also sometimes outfitted with quarter boots, little cups to protect the back of the front hooves.

But his reputation as a horse who needed little or no equipment beyond a harness to attach him to the sulky began during those training miles in Cleveland. It became part of the legend.

After nearly thirty years of experience with horses who disappointed more often than they lived up to expectations, Myron

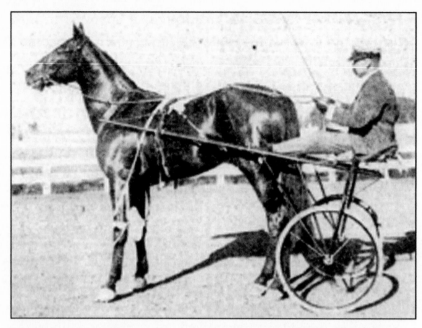

Among the earliest known photographs of Dan Patch with Myron McHenry in the sulky. *(Photo: New York Daily Tribune October 16, 1901)*

McHenry didn't want to acknowledge just how much excitement he was feeling about his new horse. Later, he would only admit to being impressed with Dan Patch's effortless speed and claimed that he had a nagging worry that the horse was too easy-going for fast competition.

But he began looking with extra care for the perfect spot for Dan Patch's debut as a big-time horse. By mid-June he suspected that he wouldn't get great odds on the horse anywhere. So he searched for the race that would present a challenge—but not too much of one—on a track that would keep him safe, on a date that would set him up for the beginning of the Grand Circuit.

He found it in Canada, an appropriate setting, considering the country's contribution to the pacing blood in Dan Patch's beautiful gait. The racetrack was in Windsor, Ontario, just across the Detroit River from the track where the Grand Circuit was to begin its 1901 season.

On Wednesday, July 10, Dan Patch jogged onto the Windsor track as the favorite in a field of six. McHenry chose a 2:15 race for his horse—at first glance a little ambitious considering that the fastest of Dan Patch's race miles the previous year had been 2:16. But there was that sub-2:10 training mile in Cleveland, and the purse was modest, just $600 for the winner. He figured it shouldn't attract too much talent. McHenry told friends that he fully expected to win.

Dan Messner also expected a win. He had made several trips to Cleveland during May and June to observe Dan Patch in training and he enthusiastically traveled to Windsor on July 8 to see his first race under the control of a professional driver.

What neither man expected was how Dan Patch did win. In the first heat he was never challenged, never urged by McHenry, never tested. The time was stunning for such an easy win: 2:07½. The second and third heats, necessary for a race victory, were nearly as fast and even easier.

The *Horse Review*, the widely read and greatly respected journal of harness racing, mentioned Dan Patch's name for the first time in the following Tuesday's edition. But it was obvious from the article that its reporters had been paying close attention in Cleveland during the spring. There had been "much curiosity," the *Review* noted, about whether Dan Patch could really be as good as he seemed.

"His performance at Windsor," the reporter added, "should satisfy these speculations pretty fully." With the eyes of both the press and the public on him, it was on to the Grand Circuit for the small town horse from Indiana.

By race day, July 17, the opportunity to place a lucrative bet had disappeared. In addition to the newspaper reports, Dan Messner was unable to control himself. While watching his horse train for the Detroit race, Messner told anyone who would listen about Dan Patch's extraordinary sense of competition and how he never would let another horse pass him, even pulling a sleigh on the snow-covered streets of Oxford.

Myron McHenry was also unable to last the week between races without a little bragging. After all, he could no longer point to the big horse's placid demeanor and claim to be worried that Dan might wilt when challenged by speedy competitors. He now knew that competition made his horse better, not worse, and that no horse entered in a 2:14 class anywhere was likely to be fast enough to beat him.

Messner and McHenry had talked in Cleveland of springing Dan Patch on an unsuspecting Grand Circuit, but on race day the chance of getting 20– or even 10–1 odds was long gone. One bookmaker offered 5–1, while others set the odds at 2–1, promising a payoff of two dollars for every dollar bet. Both Messner and McHenry placed wagers, but they both suspected that the purse money was going to be more rewarding than what they might take from their bookmakers. Most important of all was what the race might do for their horse's reputation.

Detroit was a prestigious venue for horses even though it was neither the highest paying nor the best attended stop on the

Grand Circuit. The Detroit Driving Club jealously guarded possession of the opening of the Circuit since it had won the dates a few years earlier, in spite of the fact that Michigan weather had an uncanny habit of unleashing torrential rainstorms on the first day of the meet almost every year.

Both the opening day and the storms had been in the custody of the club since the 1880s, when their racetrack was located in the nearby village of Hamtramck. That track had proved to be too small, too slow, and not nearly stylish enough for the wealthy people who supported racing.

In 1894 the Club moved operations northeast to the shores of Lake St. Clair in Grosse Pointe, already a fashionable suburb of the increasingly dirty and crowded city. Summer homes of Detroit's wealthiest people hugged the shoreline in Grosse Pointe and members decided to locate their track in a convenient place.

The racetrack they built was magnificent, with clean and comfortable seating suitable for ladies as well as the men who usually frequented tracks. Much of the seating was under cover, designed with mid-July's inevitable rain in mind. The Grosse Pointe track also included a couple of elegant restaurants and space for an orchestra to entertain between races. A private trolley line connected the track to the city of Detroit for spectators not fortunate enough to own summer homes in Grosse Pointe.

Most important was the track itself, a mile long oval of well-groomed dirt, perfectly engineered to allow the horses to sweep around the turns without interference or danger. The club had spent so much money constructing its beautiful facility that the organization now teetered on the brink of bankruptcy, but their track was so admired that it had caught the eye of a local man who readily admitted to despising horses.

Henry Ford, thirty-eight years old in 1901, had been born and raised on a farm a few miles away. As a boy he was dragged by a team of plow horses and vowed never to farm as an adult. He had, in spite of his vow, but by July of 1901 he'd managed to leave farming and had been supporting his family with a series of engineering jobs.

In 1899 Ford had talked twelve investors into giving him $150,000 for the Detroit Automobile Company, which would build a gasoline-powered delivery wagon of his own design. In early 1901 the company folded, but Ford was convinced that the problem was less that the world didn't want a horseless wagon and more that it hadn't heard about it.

Henry Ford noted the attention lavished upon the Grand Circuit racing in Grosse Pointe and certainly made note of the quality of the track's design. As soon as the Circuit left town, Ford and friends began negotiating with the Detroit Driving Club for the use of the track for an automobile race, an event that he was sure would draw attention to his new venture, the Ford Motor Company.

He was right. In the October race, Ford drove his own twenty-six-horsepower, two-cylinder car to victory in a ten-mile race. The competition drew fewer fans than the Grand Circuit races, about 8,000, but it got the attention Ford craved.

If Myron McHenry heard about the Detroit engineer's covetous looks at the track, he wouldn't have worried about what it meant to the future of harness racing, or the future of horses for that matter. But he would have worried about what the use of racetracks by automobiles would do to the condition of the racing surface.

By the time he jogged Dan Patch onto the track for the first heat of his first Grand Circuit race, McHenry was convinced that nothing but bad luck or a poor racing surface would defeat his horse. He was happy to discover no problems with the track. Ruts from speeding automobiles were to be made three months in the future.

Remarkably, the weather presented no problem either, an excellent omen to spectators and horsemen. Nor did McHenry have problems with the rest of the field. In spite of the presence of two respectable pacers, Captain Sphinx and Amorel, Dan Patch won three straight heats with no serious competition.

The win was more impressive than the victory in Windsor, even though Dan Patch didn't go as fast in any of the heats in Grosse Pointe as he did in the first heat in Canada. McHenry and Messner congratulated each other that each of the three heats was timed in less than 2:10 (not the case in Windsor). And, besides, it was the Grand Circuit.

But Dan Patch remained a secret of racing insiders, although certainly a poorly kept one. In Grosse Pointe, as in most of the other stops of the Grand Circuit that summer, much of the public attention was lavished on Cresceus, a headstrong red horse of spectacular speed and talent, the fastest trotting stallion in history. Cresceus lowered his own world record for a stallion the day after Dan Patch's race and was poised to break the overall record. Never mind, Myron McHenry told Dan Messner. Their turn at a world record would come, and not so far in the future either.

Messner sent a telegram home to Oxford, where Daniel Senior had remained to keep the store open and perhaps pick up some extra sales to people who dropped by to ask about news from Detroit. When the telegram arrived, Daniel stepped outside with the report that half the town seemed to be waiting for.

A cheer arose around the Oxford town square when Daniel told them that the equine Dan had won, then rose to a higher level when he read out the times of the three heats. It seemed inconceivable to the people gathered across from Messner and Son that a horse foaled in little Oxford could be capable of such speed.

There's no record of John Wattles waiting at Messner's to hear the news. Throughout his life, Wattles remained proud of the horse's accomplishments, but he did have some lingering resentment of losing the training job.

Dan Junior, still wearing the jaunty summer straw hat that he had sported in fashionable Grosse Pointe, arrived back in Oxford on Saturday, four days after the race, while McHenry shipped Dan Patch back to Cleveland. On Saturday night, friends began knocking on the Messners' door, while more casual acquaintances waited until Sunday morning, all of them hoping to learn unreported details of the Grand Circuit race. Dan Messner was happy to oblige. He was also pleased to include the particulars in his weekly ad for Messner and Son, as he did nearly every week throughout that first summer on the Grand Circuit.

By Monday, Messner was back in Cleveland to rejoin the Grand Circuit, ready to watch his horse compete on Tuesday, over what was now his home track, in another 2:14 class. It was one more three-heat victory as the heavy favorite. "No more than a stiff jog for Dan Patch," wrote one journalist.

Again it was Cresceus who got most of the public attention, thanks to his new world record in the more highly publicized open trot later in the week. But Dan Patch's reputation continued to grow, and not just among the well informed.

"Look out for Dan Patch," proclaimed the cryptic, single-sentence paragraph at the top of a *Horse Review* column the next week. The secret was out in a big way, and Dan Messner noticed the difference. Spectators pointed and cheered, newspapermen asked his opinion, and bookmakers crowded the rails for training miles.

But Messner especially noticed the difference in the company he was keeping. He may have been one of the richest men in Oxford, Indiana, but he had discovered on his first trip to the Cleveland track in May that his entire bank account wasn't much more than pocket change for some of the men now casting admiring glances toward Dan Patch.

These men were following a fifty-year tradition of depositing some of the millions they made in commodities, natural resources, and shipping into the pockets of breeders and trainers of harness horses. Dan Messner might have met Harold M. Hanna in the spring during the training weeks at the Glenville track, since Hanna would have made it a point to check out the new horse in the McHenry barn as well as the man paying the horse's bills. But now, with the Grand Circuit underway, the Great Lakes shipbuilder was probably paying extra attention to the shopkeeper from Oxford. What's more, H. M. Hanna may have introduced Dan Messner to his equally rich and far more illustrious brother as soon as the Circuit reached Cleveland the third week in July.

Senator Mark Hanna had arrived home shortly after the Fourth of July, as soon as President McKinley left Washington for his own home in Canton, Ohio. Hanna and McKinley had been nearly inseparable since 1891, when Hanna signed on as campaign manager for then-Congressman McKinley's run for Ohio governor. The rich and rough Mark Hanna greatly admired the easygoing and likeable McKinley, while McKinley saw in Hanna a man who shared his business-oriented conservatism and possessed an understanding of grass roots politics.

Sugar tycoon C. J. Hamlin didn't like pacers but finally realized that the rest of America did. *(Photo: Munsey's Magazine December 1904)*

The two had achieved the Ohio governorship for McKinley, followed by two successful races for the Presidency. Each felt he deserved a couple of months in Ohio, McKinley to rest in his modest Canton house and Hanna to entertain in his lavish Cleveland mansion while attending some of the Grand Circuit races. McKinley did plan a visit to Cleveland to stay with Hanna, although, not being much of a racing man, he scheduled it for the second week in September.

Sadly, the visit never took place. Just before traveling to Cleveland in September, McKinley made a quick side trip to Buffalo for a Hanna-approved appearance at the popular Pan-American Exposition. While greeting well-wishers on September 6, 1901, he was shot by anarchist Leon Frank Czolgosz, the Detroit-born son of a Polish immigrant farmer. Mark Hanna rushed to McKinley's bedside but his aid and support was not enough this time and the president died a week later.

In a bit of irony that wouldn't be appreciated until later, the Circuit itself moved to Buffalo after a stop in Columbus. There Dan Messner heard a great deal about—and possibly met—another of the harness racing barons, a man even richer than the Hannas.

He was Cicero Jabez Hamlin, builder of the Buffalo Driving Park and owner of Village Farm, home to eight hundred of the finest Standardbreds in the world. Hamlin was the Sugar King, the man who had all but cornered the market on glucose through his Buffalo Grape Sugar Company.

C. J. Hamlin was reputed to be the richest man in New York outside Manhattan and he had used a good part of his money on fast trotters. He didn't much care for pacers, even though he had relented when he paid $10,000 for a pacing stallion named Direct Hal. He had been talked into buying a couple of other good pacers too. Hamlin was enough of a businessman to know that people loved seeing fast pacers and that buyers of young horses had begun looking for them. He himself believed that only handsome trotters were worthwhile.

Hamlin's prejudice existed in spite of his own history of self-creation, having arrived in western New York as a seventeen-year clerk in his brother's grocery store. A few months later he bought the business, expanded to dry goods, then to sugar. He was a million-aire in 1868 when he turned his attention to racehorses.

His goal at his Village Farm was to breed the best trotters in the world, and he would do that by following two principles. One was that the handsomest horses would produce the fastest offspring. Foolish on its face, this principle proved to have some merit. A determined individual horse might overcome badly shaped legs or a back of the wrong length, but a son or daughter who inherited the problem might not be able to do so.

His second guiding principle was that extreme speed was all that mattered in breeding stock. Stamina was admirable, good nature was pleasant, determination was useful. But all paled in comparison to speed. He had no interest in breeding a lot of horses who were pretty good, even though he and others might make a living from them.

"I would rather produce one 2:10 trotter than a hundred that could go in 2:30," he would say to anybody who would listen. A lot of people listened to a man who was worth $15 million and willing to spend a good chunk of it on racehorses.

Hamlin was nearly eighty-one when Dan Patch first came to Buffalo, and he left no record of whether he got to the racetrack on August 8. He may well have, since his promising young pacer Shadow Chimes appeared a couple of races before Dan Patch's event. He might have chosen not to make the effort to see a pacer, even his own, especially since Buffalo's 1901 Grand Circuit races were held on the Canadian side of Lake Erie.

If Hamlin had made the trip, he would have seen exactly what he admired in a horse. The handsome Dan Patch demonstrated pure speed that day like few people in the record crowd had ever seen. Cicero Hamlin would also have enjoyed a demonstration worthy of a titan of industry. In this case, though, the demonstration came at the hand of a titan of the racetrack.

Myron McHenry was so confident that he tried what he hoped would be a secret test, although it was one he would conduct in full view of thousands of racing fans. It would be done, he decided, to assure himself of Dan Patch's true quality. And it would be fun. He may have also been trying to one-up Shadow Chimes, who had paced a fast time in the earlier race.

Dan Patch, who had managed to remain qualified for the 2:14 class, raced on Thursday, August 8, against several of the same horses he'd been facing since July. McHenry had no reason to believe that the result would be any different and fully expected short odds and three straight heat wins.

The record crowd expected the same and got it: three comfortable wins. The times for the three miles were unimpressive for an improving young horse on a hot dry day: 2:17¼, 2:10¾, and 2:14½. The total for the three was by far the slowest of any of Dan Patch's three-heat races on the Grand Circuit, and even the second heat, the fastest of the three, didn't approach his best time of the season.

The casual fans rationalized that a good horse only has to go as fast as he needs to go to win, although some acknowledged disappointment. They also admitted surprise when they heard McHenry's comments to a group of newspapermen.

"This horse," McHenry said, with a gesture towards Dan Patch, "is the best pacer I've ever drawn a rein over." McHenry, although always ready with a good quote, was not so inclined to use the word "best" lightly. He had other owners to think about.

While casual fans might have been surprised that seemingly average times could draw such enthusiasm out of a man who'd sat behind some of the best pacers in recent decades, the journalists and the more knowledgeable fans nodded in agreement. They knew they had seen something extraordinary.

Instead of following the most basic rule of racing a dominant horse—get to the lead at the start and improve your position—Myron McHenry had deliberately pulled Dan Patch to last place in the first heat. With a horse that easily tires, or one whose quality may be suspect, that's good strategy. The horse doesn't work too hard too early, and he gets a little help from the other horses blocking the wind in front of him.

None of that was necessary with Dan Patch. What Myron McHenry did was give his horse the hardest possible test. When McHenry loosened his grip at the top of the stretch, allowing Dan to pace as fast as he wanted to for the final quarter mile, he came up with a thirty second quarter. And that, everybody knew, was a two-minute mile pace.

McHenry had been telling Dan Messner for months that his horse could become a two-minute miler. Messner had been happy to hear it, but skeptical. When McHenry repeated the promise after the three heats in Buffalo, he had that 30 second quarter to back it up. If Dan Patch could carry that speed over a mile, he would join a very short list of two-minute performers. In August 1901 the list consisted of one horse: Star Pointer.

Shortly after the Buffalo appearance, Myron McHenry loaded Dan Patch onto a train for New York, with Messner following in another train. McHenry had been there before and knew what to expect, but Dan Messner and Dan Patch were about to find themselves in a place difficult to fathom for a man and horse from small-town Indiana.

The next Grand Circuit stop was scheduled for Brighton Beach at Coney Island. It was a place where money and mayhem often collided, and—although the mayhem wasn't always present—the money certainly was. The trip to Brighton Beach marked the beginning of a chain of events that would eventually leave both Dan Messner and Myron McHenry by the wayside and propel Dan Patch to an unthinkable level of fame and fortune.

8

THE BIG STAGE

MYRON MCHENRY SHOULD have known better. He had been sucked into the whirlpool of New York racing several times over the past few years and knew how easily horsemen could drown in what New York had to offer: money, status, and fame—but mostly money. McHenry had emerged more or less unscathed and he relished the idea of coming back with a fast, new horse that he could show off to people who mattered.

Harness racing existed in New York at the turn of the last century because people who mattered wanted it there. It was an odd turnabout for the sport and the city. In the early nineteenth century, when trotting races were first recorded, New York was the center of the racing world. Farmers, livery operators, deliverymen, and others who thought they had the fastest horse around usually took that horse to New York to prove it.

In 1806 a trotter named Yankey from either New Haven or Boston (newspaper reports vary but New England was clearly involved) traveled to Harlem to show his talents, and he trotted history's first recorded sub-three minute mile. In 1817 Boston Blue, who really was from Boston, surprised New Yorkers by defeating a local star in the country's first notable head-to-head trotting competition.

By mid-century, the most famous harness horse in the country was a gray mare from Long Island who was supposedly discovered pulling an oyster wagon. That was Lady Suffolk, whose crown was usurped a few years later by Flora Temple. The bob-tailed Flora was spotted trailing a drove of beef cattle to market in New York, having been brought along because her upstate owner couldn't find a buyer at home for his ill-behaved little mare. There were plenty of prominent horses and owners whose blood was considerably bluer, but the compelling narrative of the era was the story of the ordinary owner with the ordinary horse who proved to be not so ordinary after all on a New York stage.

Then rich men (extremely rich ones) discovered the joys of harness racing and the story changed. First, Cornelius Vanderbilt decided that the wealthiest man in the country deserved to drive the fastest trotters. His rival Robert Bonner, the millionaire owner of the *New York Ledger*, bought his first trotting horse in 1856 and the race was on. Ordinary was no longer such a desirable description of either horse or owner.

Between them, Vanderbilt and Bonner spent hundreds of thousands on trotting horses, and their spending lured other well-heeled New Yorkers into the sport. By the 1870s the top level of New York harness racing was almost exclusively in the hands of the rich and powerful. There was little room for anybody else, and many of the owners didn't much care if only their friends saw their good horses.

Racetracks came and went, but the reins of the best horses were in the hands of wealthy owners who preferred to compete on city streets: on Broadway and Third Avenue, and the Jamaica Road out to Long Island. They didn't like racetracks, believing them to be in the hands of riffraff.

But the rise of the middle class, while it helped the harness racehorse in the Midwest, made it almost impossible for New York's leisure drivers to compete at speed on their favorite routes. There were too many cabs and delivery wagons and window-shopping pedestrians in the way.

In 1880 an organization of well-to-do owners leased the handsome Fleetwood Park, built in 1871 on the grounds of the Revolutionary War–era Morris estate in the Bronx. Fleetwood was well suited to Vanderbilts and Bonners as it featured an elegant French Second Empire clubhouse and a grandstand that curved as gracefully as the racetrack did. No riffraff were involved. Only organization members and friends were allowed in, although members did hire professional drivers like Myron McHenry to handle some of their horses.

Late in 1897 Fleetwood Park succumbed to the pressure of residential development and there was no longer organized harness competition in New York City. The wealthy owners hadn't really wanted a racetrack anyway, and if they got the private speedway they really wanted, Fleetwood Park would become another, although somewhat greener, subdivision. The gentlemen drivers first hoped to have the city build them a speedway in Central Park, but the outcry over the potential loss to the public of a big chunk of their open space stopped that plan in its tracks.

Instead, New York taxpayers supplied the driving enthusiasts with a magnificent stretch of raceway in northern Manhattan, along the west bank of the Harlem River. This was the two-and-a-half mile Speedway, opened to great fanfare in 1898. The project had the backing of Tammany Hall, the Democratic organization that ran city government. The support was necessary, given the taxpayer-funded cost of about five million dollars. The

The Harlem River Speedway hosted the wealthy of New York as they raced their trotters and pacers. (Photo: Library of Congress)

wealthy horsemen were thrilled, particularly when the city agreed that riders, bicyclists, and pedestrians were not permitted, even when racing was not going on.

Ordinary admirers of fast horses could watch the Speedway races (although from a distance and with little idea of who was competing), but one group of New Yorkers was conspicuously left out. Given their power and money, these men were not inclined to be overlooked. Professional gamblers, particularly those who ran horse-betting operations, wanted organized racing. They were unimpressed with competitions between gentlemen in which it wasn't even clear whose dark bay horse was racing against whose chestnut mare.

There were several Thoroughbred tracks in New York, but many professional gamblers preferred harness racing, and not just because they liked to see horses compete under harness. By the turn of the century, a Thoroughbred race consisted of just one heat. The field would race for the specified eight furlongs (one mile) or ten furlongs and the first horse across the finish line was the winner.

In harness racing heats still ruled, with two or three wins required for a victory. That meant more and increasingly complex bets, which in turn meant more money to be won or lost. It also meant a greater chance of fraud, because a horse could lose a heat and still win a race. It was the racing equivalent of having your cake and eating it too. It was generally understood that professional drivers of the era were able to sample a lot of cake.

In 1898 Tammany stalwart William H. Clark, former corporation counsel for the city, spent at least half a million dollars of his own money (or more likely taxpayer money) to build a beautiful new track, which he named Empire City, in the suburbs near Yonkers. Clark's illness and death early in 1900 led to the sale of the track.

For a few months, it appeared that Frank Farrell was the successful buyer, proving just how much professional gamblers really did want organized harness racing in New York. Farrell was known as the "poolroom king" because he was thought to own an interest in as many as 250 of the 300 New York houses that offered auction pools for gambling on horse racing. In addition, Farrell owned all or part of a number of casinos, including several of the most lucrative and luxurious.

But the wealthy kings of racing thought that Farrell's ownership of Empire City was a little unseemly, even though most of them knew Frank Farrell and many patronized his higher-end gambling establishments. Instead, a group headed by grocery store magnate James Butler, an amateur driver, enthusiastic gambler, and former employer of Myron McHenry, was permitted to buy the track. Professional baseball saw nothing unseemly about Farrell. Shortly after his Empire City failure, he imported a team of the new American Baseball League from Baltimore. It was eventually named the New York Yankees.

Butler himself may not have been so pristine. Although he was never identified as a gambling house owner, he did maintain business relationships with men who emphatically were. But appearances counted, and Butler's canned goods appeared to be a more legitimate source of money than roulette wheels.

Empire City offered no Grand Circuit races in 1901. While they waited to take possession of the new track Butler and others leased the Brighton Beach Thoroughbred track in the Gravesend section of Brooklyn for Grand Circuit racing in August.

The gambling fraternity felt right at home in the vacation atmosphere of Brighton Beach. Dan Patch was to appear in his first East Coast race in front of thousands of spectators, some of whom would wander over from the boardwalk and beach at neighboring Coney Island, and hundreds of professional gamblers who would be there to make a little money. Myron McHenry, who knew many of the gamblers from previous visits, would get more than he bargained for, although he didn't realize it for some time.

Dan Patch's race was scheduled for the end of the meet. That was a little late for McHenry, so he offered his horse's services in a way that was guaranteed to get attention: as a workmate for his own sire. Joe Patchen now stood at stud in upstate New York and was scheduled to begin his summer job as a racehorse on the opening day of the Brighton Beach meet.

It was an ambitious and public way for Dan Patch to get used to the clamor and commotion of New York. He did his job flawlessly, pacing alongside his famous sire. Joe Patchen later in the day proved to be out of condition, losing his race, but Dan Patch's appearance did make the newspapers. One reporter described him as a "magnificent natural gaited pacer, as steady as clockwork and with the speed of the wind." At one level at least, Dan Patch had made it in New York.

The four-day delay between the training appearance and the race gave Dan Messner time to visit business acquaintances in the city, people from whom he had bought fabric and shoes and buttons for the Messner store. It gave Myron McHenry time to renew acquaintances with another kind of businessman, and nobody knows even today if the combination of time, circumstance, and doubtful company led to the bizarre event that took place when New Yorkers got their first look at Dan Patch.

By the late afternoon of August 16 the weather at Brighton Beach was sultry and sunny, with very little breeze blowing in off the Atlantic. Since harness horses tend to race fastest in hot weather, both professionals and fans expected fast times in a straight three-heat win from a horse they'd been hearing about. They had been reading in the *Times* and the *World* about the new wonder horse from Indiana and they already knew about Myron McHenry. He was just the kind of no-holds-barred driver well appreciated by rowdy New Yorkers.

The professionals had better sources. In this case, at least one of them got the story, if not from the horse's mouth, from the next best thing. Myron McHenry had met Manley E. Sturges, a Manhattan casino manager and owner, while driving James Butler-owned horses for the prominent trainer Thomas Keating. Keating had died unexpectedly in the fall of 1900, leaving a will that offered, among other things, a modest bequest to all women who showed up claiming to be the Widow Keating.

Upon receiving the news (of Keating's death, not the possibility of multiple widows) Butler had announced that he was getting out of the horse ownership business. That turned out to be temporary, but in the meantime, his friend Manley Sturges maintained a relationship with both Butler and Keating's favorite driver, Myron McHenry.

In the hours before Dan Patch's first New York race, Sturges won an auction pool on him with a wager of $1300. This was ten times the highest bid on any horse in any other race of the day. Sturges stood to more than double his money on the pool on the final result of the three-heat race, not an individual heat.

James Butler, friend of Sturges and former employer of McHenry, bet heavily in other pools, as did Nick Hubinger of New Haven, Connecticut, a wealthy manufacturer of something called "elastic starch." Hubinger was a horse owner and a heavy gambler who was an acquaintance and probably a client of Sturges. They stayed out of the Dan Patch race but may have bet elsewhere.

For those who failed to win a pool, there was betting at bookmaker stalls at the track and at gambling houses in the city, but the bookmakers gave odds for each heat, not just the entire race. Dan Patch was heavily favored for the first heat and the full race at all venues.

Bookmakers set odds individually and the figures were not automatically readjusted depending on the money wagered as they are today. Although the initial bookmaker odds on the first heat were 3-5 on Dan Patch, providing for only a modest return, they had increased to 5-4 by race time, and a win would have given a handsome payoff on what looked to be a sure thing. The New York *World* reported the next day that there had been a "mad scramble" for tickets at these generous odds and the money poured into the bookmakers' moneybags.

Sturges's business partner Sol Lichtenstein was the most respected odds maker at New York tracks at that time and the other bookmakers tended to follow his lead. Sturges was not known to be a bookmaker himself, but the business relationship with Lichtenstein may have enabled him to share in any money taken in but not paid out. At the very least, he would have known what was going on, if indeed anything was.

What did happen was this: The start of the first heat was delayed by nearly an hour by a racehorse named Paul Revere, whose equipment failed repeatedly. That problem was sorted out, but the start was ragged anyway. Not to worry, Dan Patch's supporters thought. Their horse, who had drawn the rail position, got away quickly and took an early lead. McHenry then eased him back on the first turn, not a typical move but still nothing to worry about.

In the homestretch, Dan Patch appeared ready to move, but McHenry gave him no more than modest encouragement. At the finish line he was fourth, beaten by Martha Marshall and two long shots. The time for the race was 2:09, nearly two seconds slower than his previous best record. On the racetrack, two seconds is an eternity.

As to what happened next, that depends on what account you believe. McHenry may have been called to the race stewards, or he may not have been. According to the *World,* the judges "who are paid because they have an expert knowledge of harness racing law" paid no attention to the improbable result. The *Boston Globe* reported that the judges were "very displeased" with the first mile. The *Atlanta Journal* claimed that it was "evident that Dan Patch was not driven to win." The *Brooklyn Eagle* noted that McHenry moved only close enough "to get a good position for him" in the lineup for the second heat.

Other reports described a heated meeting between McHenry and the stewards and a near riot on the part of fans. McHenry told anyone who would listen that he had heard that Martha

Marshall was fast and he had only wanted to see just how fast. He held back to see how things sorted themselves out and the finish, he claimed, came a little too soon.

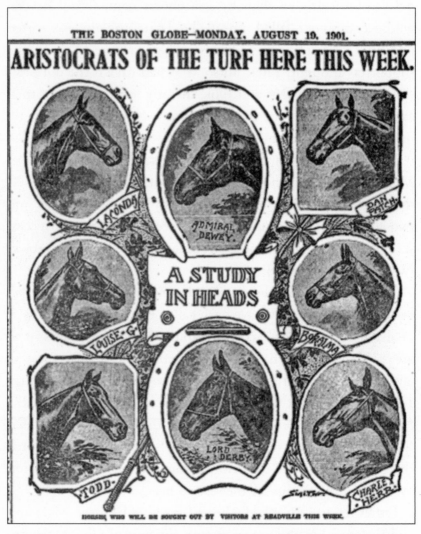

Dan Patch became one of the "Aristocrats of the Turf" in August 1901.
(Boston Globe August 19, 1901)

Manley Sturges, whose big bet was on the race, not the heat, was unperturbed. Whether McHenry was embarrassed at his poor judgment of pace (as he claimed) or felt that he'd been a little too obvious (as the fans and reporters believed) in the first heat, he was all business in the second. He drove Dan Patch to a mile in 2:04½, beating his own best time ever by nearly two seconds, and improving on the first heat by four and a half seconds, a millennium in racing terms. More exciting to spectators was the announcement that one of the quarter miles had been timed in just a fraction over thirty seconds.

Because of the delay in the opening heat and the tumult between the first and second, the race could not be finished before dark and was carried over to the next day. In the third and fourth heats, there was no sorting out, no easing back, nothing but speed from Dan Patch. The third heat featured a comfortable win over the field in 2:07¼, and the fourth—a race off with Martha Marshall—was an easy and fast victory in 2:05¾. Officially, Dan Patch was still undefeated.

Dan Messner must have been happy but a bit mystified by what had happened at Brighton Beach. It was exhilarating to own a horse admired by even the most jaded New Yorkers. This pleasure helped him suppress an uneasy feeling that he might be in over his head. It also allowed him to turn down the first big-money offer for his horse, whispered to be $20,000. It was an unlikely figure for a pacer, whose earning potential was still limited. Gossip said the offer came from Manley Sturges, who had won a lot of money on the Brighton Beach race.

McHenry packed up his horse, his sulky, and his training cart and caught a train to the suburbs of Boston, where harness racing had enjoyed an unbroken run for nearly a hundred years. It was a city where people dearly loved their trotters and pacers.

On August 18 the *Boston Globe* printed a picture of Dan Patch for the first time, as one of the "aristocrats of the turf" scheduled to appear the following week at Readville, in the Hyde Park neighborhood of Boston. The reporter noted that he appeared to be several classes above the horses he would face and that

Rhode Island's Narragansett Trotting Park was one of the most prestigious racing venues in the country and the site of Dan Patch's first bow to the crowd. *(Photo: Library of Congress)*

the results would be "as close as McHenry cares to draw the finishes."

He and the horse would have a special advantage at the Readville Trotting Park. Hopples were not permitted by track regulations, so hoppled pacers like Martha Marshall were not around to challenge him. Nor was there legal betting on his race, possibly because of the peculiarities at Brighton Beach. But it was a well-designed mile track, in excellent condition, and a likely spot for McHenry to further impress easterners.

The August 22 event was a routine three heat win for Dan Patch, so uneventful that a group of little girls who were dancing happily in the stands drew nearly as many eyes as the heats. It was on to Cranston, Rhode Island, for the next stop on the Grand Circuit, at the Narragansett Trotting Park.

Appropriately, the track stood very near where colonial Rhode Islanders developed the Narragansett Pacer into the first uniquely American horse breed, one whose blood probably remained in the veins of every pacing racehorse, including Dan Patch. Governor William Sprague, a Civil War hero and wealthy industrialist, had originally built the track for the private use of his horses. Now it was one of the most admired racetracks in the country, convenient to visitors from both Boston and Manhattan.

The race, scheduled for August 30, proved to be unexpectedly challenging. Dan Patch had reached that midpoint of fame where he didn't yet scare away all opposition. Instead, he lured ambitious horsemen to take a chance for the fame that might come with beating him. A mare named Mazette pushed him to a 2:04½ mile in the first heat, and in the second, McHenry was forced to urge him actively—an unprecedented necessity—but

Ren Nash, who gave Dan Patch his "French ladies' shoes," enjoyed fishing as well as making custom horseshoes. *(Photo: International Stock Food Farm Yearbook 1906)*

he prevailed. The third heat was easier.

Far from alarming McHenry, the performances thrilled him. Although he had failed to mention it publicly, his horse had been coughing earlier in the week and was nowhere near fully fit for the race. If Dan Patch could race 2:04½ in poor health, the sky really was the limit.

People at the trotting track that day insisted they saw Dan Patch make amends for his subpar performance by making a deep bow to the crowd before being led away. It may have been something else: an itch scratched, an effort to find a little grass, or a jump at a shadow. It may have been imagined. Or maybe Dan Patch had really learned to acknowledge the crowd. Whichever was true, the crowd reacted with delight and he and McHenry would remember the reaction. Dan Patch was on his way to becoming one of the most beloved athletes in the history of American sports.

At the next stop on the circuit, Hartford, Connecticut's splendid Charter Oak Park, Myron McHenry was so calm and confident (and perhaps so disappointed) that he could no longer make any money betting on Dan Patch, that he drove other horses in two other races on September 5—a total of ten heats for the day. He failed to win with the other horses, but he did earn a little extra cash.

Dan Patch's race consisted of another three wins in three heats, although the times weren't impressive. He had reached still another level: the bittersweet one where winning isn't good enough, and his human family was a little disappointed.

A slow but routine three-heat win in Cincinnati on September 21 was followed by two weeks of rest and readjustment for Myron McHenry and Dan Patch. In harness racing, if a horse disappoints with no obvious physical reason for it, you adjust the equipment. Messner and McHenry—and John Wattles before—had been proud of the limited equipment required by their horse. Even the newspaper reporters back east had noted how fast and how securely he could go with simple rigging.

He didn't need hopples—and still didn't because he never put a foot wrong in his gait—but now McHenry again had his shoes adjusted, this time by a farrier named Ren Nash. The toes were shortened even more, and the heels lifted further by the shoes. Reporters began to notice the "French ladies' shoes" that became part of his legend.

Observers noted that the new shoes didn't improve his gait, which was already a thing of beauty, but they did seem to return some zest to his racing style. On October 1 he surprised everyone except perhaps McHenry by completing a routine, non-competitive training mile in Lexington, Kentucky, in 2:04. The last quarter came in at less than thirty seconds and the two minute mile became tantalizingly closer.

The Lexington track did permit betting the following week on Dan's return to real racing, but nobody expected much profit. The pool bought a bid of $200 on Dan Patch and a total bid of $25 on the rest of the field. Whoever won that pool didn't earn much when Dan reeled off three straight heats. The first two heats were timed in 2:05½ and 2:05.

The final race of Dan Patch's 1901 season was to take place during the first meet ever held at a track intended to be perfect. The Memphis Driving Park had been built over the summer and early fall by a designer who enjoyed an open checkbook, thanks to Chicago millionaire Cornelius K. G. Billings, who was an excellent amateur driver and an even better purchaser of fine horses.

Billings had made his millions in gas and coal and spread the money around on railways, city trolley companies, and harness racehorses. He managed to combine the latter two when he commissioned the Memphis track early in 1901, with a goal of hosting the final Grand Circuit meeting of the year. Billings rationalized that people would use his Memphis Street Railway Company to visit the track, so it made perfect business sense to spend hundreds of thousands of dollars to bring in all those five cent fares.

Billings hired Seth Griffin, builder and superintendent of the Readville track in Massachusetts, to build him the fastest harness track in the world. He obliged. A man who liked to dress like a British explorer with pipe and cap, Griffin also included fourteen modern stable buildings, spacious grandstands, and two comfortable clubhouses. Billings added a golf course in the infield, although presumably he didn't expect flying golf balls while the races were actually underway.

Proof that the new track was indeed fast came early and often during the six-day Grand Circuit meet that began October 21. Dan Patch's performance should have been overshadowed by the horses who challenged and exceeded world records. He was still competing in the 2:08 category for less experienced horses and, although he won in straight heats, his best time was just 2:05—good but hardly a record.

But after the race, Dan Patch performed what was becoming one of the most eagerly anticipated events in racing when he bowed to the thousands of people in the stands. His name was mentioned prominently in every review of the Memphis meet.

The Grand Circuit of 1901 was over, and Myron McHenry gave Dan Messner permission to take Dan Patch home to Indiana. His horse had left Oxford in the early spring to modest fanfare carrying the hopes of his community along with him. He returned to an exuberant hometown celebration carrying along a different kind of attention: admiring, curious, and sometimes greedy eyes from across the country.

The people of Oxford were well aware that other eyes were on them and they were determined to show that they deserved to possess a horse of Dan Patch's caliber. He arrived by train on November 2, greeted by nearly 200 people who were convinced that the horse knew he was home. When the car door opened, he looked out, raised his head, and nickered to the crowd. They said he knew precisely the way to his old stall.

Twelve days later, they gave him the homecoming celebration they'd been planning for months. The Oxford town band marched through the square playing a "Dan Patch Two-Step", one of several that would eventually be written. They were followed by Dan Patch under harness, in glowing good health in spite of a long racing season, and members of his equine family: his yearling daughter Lady Patch, his dam Zelica, and her two more recent foals, both half brothers to Dan himself. Hundreds of people crowded the square to see, and thousands more were able to read about the event in newspapers in distant cities. One admirer in particular was paying close attention.

9

A GAMBLER TAKES A CHANCE

MANLEY EDWIN STURGES was a man who hungered to be something he wasn't. The career he chose as a young man in upstate New York had been good to him, but he now wanted more than a large bank account. By 1901 chasing money held less satisfaction than it had before, partly due to problems in his profession but also because of a decades-old yearning. His seven-month campaign to buy Dan Patch was part of a long-term effort at personal reinvention.

Sturges wanted as few people as possible to know where he came from, how he had $20,000 to buy a horse, and why he wanted a famous horse anyway. His name itself was difficult to pin down. He appears in newspapers of the time as Manley (the correct spelling), Manly, or even Warley. His last name is more often spelled Sturgis than Sturges (which was correct), and even appears as Storgess and Sturgess. He succeeded so well in masking

Manley E. Sturges, Manhattan casino operator and big-time gambler, was Dan Patch's second owner. *(Photo: Horse Review June 1921)*

the truth that upon his death twenty years later, many of his obituaries were illustrated with the picture of another man.

The mask didn't lift after his death. Even today, with our computerized databases of genealogy and vital statistics, his private life and business dealings are obscured by a spider's web of broken links and loose ends.

At the time it became widely known that he was the deep-pocketed, potential buyer of Dan Patch. Manley Sturges was described as an elderly bachelor from Buffalo, sometimes identified as a capitalist and a broker. He wasn't elderly. Even in 1901, a fifty-one year old man was not elderly. He wasn't a bachelor, although he kept his wife well hidden. He wasn't from Buffalo, although he had worked there for a couple of years in his twenties. To call him a broker was to stretch the definition, although he certainly was a capitalist.

At the time he began his quest for Dan Patch, Manley Sturges was the operator and part owner of one of the most luxurious casinos in Manhattan, a profession that was completely illegal and extraordinarily lucrative. He did gamble himself, but what he risked at auction pools and with bookmakers was a fraction of what he took in from other gamblers. The lavish surroundings of the roulette wheels and faro tables at the Victoria Club at 15 West 32nd Street were matched by only two other gambling houses in New York: Richard Canfield's legendary casino on West 44th and Frank Farrell's opulent House with the Bronze Doors a block away from the Victoria on West 33rd.

Sturges was a practiced casino operator. Since his arrival in Manhattan a decade earlier he had weathered police raids, half a dozen official investigations, and several economic downturns, managing to remain rich and nearly anonymous throughout. As far as can be determined, he was never taken away from the Victoria or his earlier clubs, the Gilsey and the Imperial, in handcuffs, never called to testify before a court or commission, and rarely mentioned in the newspapers in connection with his real profession.

His first Manhattan job was as resident manager of the mid-level Gilsey Club at 21 West 31st Street. He may have been an employee, or he may have been part owner. Syndicates usually owned the gambling clubs and their precise makeup was both fluid and unpublicized.

Sturges came to Manhattan in about 1890 with experience in the legal and illegal hospitality industry and with a bankroll made from managing and partly owning the legal Bayshore Hotel on Sodus Bay on Lake Ontario. Much more money came in from an undefined interest in the nearby Pavilion, a restaurant and store that offered illegal gambling in a back room. The nominal owner of in the Pavilion was George Emery, a well-connected Republican official. Sturges had no legal problems with either the Bayshore or the Pavilion and learned a valuable lesson about the usefulness of political relationships.

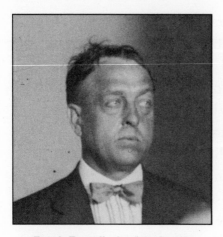

Frank Farrell, the "poolroom king" of New York, was a business partner of Manley Sturges. He was among the early owners of the New York Yankees franchise. (Photo: Library of Congress)

If Sturges did buy a piece of the action at the Gilsey, he most likely did so from Frank Farrell, who years later tried to buy the Empire City track after making himself the most prominent of the gambling operators in the city. Farrell was revealed as the primary partner in the Gilsey property a few years later, but it's not clear when he actually acquired it. The original incorporators, who filed papers for a gentlemen's club in 1887, did not include Farrell but did include several of his associates. It was well known that Farrell never, if he could possibly avoid it, owned anything outright. He was willing to spread the profits if he could also spread the risks, and a gambling club provided substantial risky profits. So Sturges may have been a partner of Frank Farrell, not just an employee.

Sturges became involved in New York racing, particularly harness racing, in about 1892. While living at the Gilsey, he purchased a few inexpensive horses and began betting on them and others. He had brought an interest in the sport with him to Manhattan. Lorenzo Whitney, a hotel operator in Sturges's hometown of Sodus, had built a half-mile track in property he owned south of the village and brief race meets had been going on since the late 1870s. Betting was strictly personal there, between friends and acquaintances.

At some point in the early nineties, possibly through his betting on races, Sturges met Sol Lichtenstein, then the most important bookmaker in the New York metropolitan area. Other men took in as much money to their books as Lichtenstein did, but none was as brilliant at setting odds.

He was a genius at adjusting odds depending on how much was being wagered on which horse. Too much coming in on one horse? Then the odds go down, encouraging bettors to look for a bigger payoff with other horses. Too little on a good horse? Then the odds get longer, assuring that more is wagered. Sol Lichtenstein, of all the dozens of bookmakers who worked the New York tracks, could set odds that would guarantee himself a good profit while satisfying his customers. Pari-mutuel computers do that easily today, but Lichtenstein did it in his head.

In 1893 Sturges, apparently with additional money from Lichtenstein, opened the Imperial Club, about a block away from the Gilsey in a four-story brownstone at 15 West 32nd Street. The club stood just outside Manhattan's notorious Tenderloin, the vice district where gambling houses competed with brothels and theatres for the city's entertainment dollars. Only the theatres were legal.

Sturges was the face of the Imperial, making himself president, but two years later Lichtenstein became more active in the operation. Lichtenstein suddenly had extra time on his hands and a growing concern about the future of his bookmaking business. Every August he and the other prominent bookmakers of New York traveled north to the village of Saratoga Springs and set up shop for the Thoroughbred race meet there.

The village, which had first come to fame as a gambling-free spa where wealthy families summered, had mixed feelings about its racetrack and the gamblers it attracted. In 1895, the voters of Saratoga Springs ousted their gambling-friendly administration and replaced it with a reform slate led by a man named Charles Sturges, who promptly spearheaded a ban on gambling.

The highly respectable Charles Sturges, lawyer and businessman, was by pure coincidence the first cousin of Manley Sturges. Manley and Charles were not close and while Manley probably knew what Charles was up to, Charles may not have known about Manley's profession. The Sturges administration lasted only two years (local merchants lost wagonloads of money when the gamblers stayed home) but the dark seasons may have prompted Sol Lichtenstein to become more active in another business.

Sturges remained manager of the Imperial. He lived in the top floor apartment on West 32nd Street without his wife. Late in 1888, the 38-year-old Sturges, then managing the Bayshore Hotel on Lake Ontario, had married the twenty-three-year-old Sarah Elizabeth Martin of nearby Lyons. She was the daughter of an Alsatian immigrant, a lock tender on the Erie Canal. Just how she came to be married to the considerably older and ambitious Sturges is a subject for speculation, but here's a possibility: the Bayshore was known for hiring good-looking "dining room girls" during the busy summer season, many of whom came from Lyons. Perhaps Sarah, known as Sadie, was one of them.

Sadie Sturges was not listed at the Imperial Club's address in city directories or census listings during the next six years, while a woman of the same name and similar age is listed as a boarder several blocks away. The couple never divorced and she survived him. But for some reason, good or bad, he chose not to live with her in on West 32nd Street.

At some point, but at least by 1899, Lichtenstein and Sturges changed both the name and the ambiance of their club. The Imperial became the Victoria, and it was reinvented as a haunt of the very rich. This was not the first time in his professional life that Manley Sturges attempted to upgrade himself.

A few years earlier, while still at the Bayshore House on Lake Ontario, he had made himself president of the Sodus Manufacturing Company, which was incorporated to mine and distribute salt. The company failed, but Sturges was able to call himself president of a business for a while and he found that he enjoyed the prestige. He apparently lost very little money in the salt venture because he soon began buying and racing yachts with men whose money was both inherited and earned. The newly christened Victoria Club provided renewed contact with the same sort of people.

Sol Lichtenstein was willing to take bets from just about anybody in the betting ring at a racetrack, but he was more particular at the Victoria Club and Manley Sturges agreed. A would-be patron had first to pass a polite, well-dressed black doorman. If approved, and approval depended on whether his manners were obvious and his money was likely, he would be admitted to the public hall on the ground floor.

This room featured specially woven carpets, rich, dark draperies that let in no outside light, and an expensive ventilation system that permitted the patrons to smoke their cigars and pipes without the necessity of opening windows. Old Masters hung on the walls and the dining tables were set with crystal and real silver. Towards the back, a selection of faro layouts, roulette wheels, and card tables saw thousands of dollars change hands in each night, with a handsome percentage retained by the house.

That amount was trivial compared to what crossed the tables nightly on the second and third floors at the Victoria. This was the private realm of serious money, where hundreds of thousands could be gambled away in a few hours. Formal records were never kept, and what we know about the size of the wagers and the men who made them comes from later accounts. Or we think we know about them.

Reginald Vanderbilt, the gambling-inclined grandson of Cornelius, was reported to have lost between $75,000 and $180,000 in a single night at a Manhattan casino, believed at the time to be the house run by Richard Canfield, the most famous of the operators. Later stories identified the Victoria as the place where the young heir dropped the money. But it's possible that both clubs benefited from the Vanderbilt largesse.

The Victoria was popular among other rich gamblers. It was almost as elegant as the two more famous clubs, Canfield's and the House with the Bronze Doors, but Sturges and Lichtenstein managed to keep the club and its patrons out of trouble. They didn't court publicity and they were apparently particularly clever in their placement of bribe money to police and politicians. The club was remarkably lucrative and rarely raided.

Something happened early in 1900 that prompted a sale of the club's valuable art works. On the auction block went seventy paintings, drawings, and sculptures, including a Gainsborough and a Brissot. Also offered, probably with Manley Sturges's regret, was a huge oil painting of Star Pointer, harness racing's first two-minute miler.

The club wasn't going out of business, and Sturges and Lichtenstein stayed on for at least a few more years as owners. Either the two men needed cash for another unrecorded purchase in 1900, or they were planning to take on a partner and didn't want their art collection included in the new man's purchase. The latter seems most likely.

At some point before 1903, probably during 1902, the legendary gambler, casino operator, and Thoroughbred racehorse owner Davey Johnson became the primary owner of the Victoria. Lichtenstein remained a partner for a few years, but apparently Sturges did not.

His willingness to leave may have been prompted by concerns about the law. In January 1901, the Victoria was one of fifteen clubs raided by police and reformers led by magistrate William Travers Jerome, whose goal was to shut down the city's gambling houses. The Victoria was least affected by the raids, having been tipped off ahead of time. Neither Sturges nor Lichtenstein (nor Johnson, for that matter) was arrested, nor were they mentioned in newspaper reports.

Jerome had no particular animus towards horse racing, coming from an important racing family. His father Lawrence and uncle Leonard Jerome were both wealthy financiers with a love of racing. Leonard built the splendid Jerome Park in the Bronx, a Thoroughbred track that hosted the best horses in the country before it closed in 1894. William Travers, for whom the magistrate was named, was a partner of both Lawrence and Leonard and was also a racing enthusiast. Travers cofounded the Saratoga track in

Magistrate William Travers Jerome, member of a famous racing family, declared war on gambling houses and may have encouraged Manley Sturges' purchase of Dan Patch. (Photo: Library of Congress)

upstate New York and lent his name to the Travers Stakes.

William Travers Jerome had impeccable family racing credentials, but waged a relentless campaign against illegal casinos and poolrooms. On the surface, there was no conflict, since track owners had long objected to off-track betting of any kind—on races or on other forms of gambling. But in pursuing casinos and poolrooms, Jerome's net also threatened to capture people involved in on-track racing, whether as bookmakers or owners.

Sturges, Lichtenstein, and Johnson may have been simply lucky enough to be elsewhere during the raids of 1901 or they may have had inside information. It's possible that Sturges had some relationship with the Jerome family, since the Jerome brothers and their wives (who were sisters) were from the same area of upstate New York near Lake Ontario. Good fortune or good connections kept Sturges out of the newspapers during the raids, but the Victoria Club itself was targeted.

It's not clear when the Victoria was actually sold to Davey Johnson, but in the summer of 1901, when Sturges began to pursue Dan Patch, it was clear he was ready to get out of the casino business and had plenty of money to pay for whatever new business he wanted to enter. The cash may have come from the gambling club, or from the sales of fine art, or from his own racetrack winnings.

It wasn't until early 1902 that his repeated offers for Dan Patch bore fruit. By this time Sturges could claim to be a sportsman, that vague and popular title of the era that could apply equally to yachtsmen and recreational gamblers.

Myron McHenry had certainly told Dan Messner something about the man who wanted to buy his horse, and he had a lot to tell. He probably had not referred to Sturges as a "sportsman." But whatever stories McHenry told, they were enough to make Messner nervous. By the time Messner had his horse back in Oxford, he had begun to see threats in Sturges's offers to buy Dan Patch, or at least so he later claimed.

Messner was not so nervous about the mysterious New Yorker who coveted Dan Patch that he kept his horse in the barn during the first weeks of 1902. Dan pulled sleigh or wagon, depending on the snow cover, nearly every day. He was visited, petted, and pointed out by everybody he passed.

Then, in mid-February, something tragic and troubling happened. Lady Patch, Dan's promising two-year-old daughter whose stall was near her sire's, suddenly became ill and died a few hours later. The first diagnosis was tetanus, a scourge of horses until vaccination became available in the 1920s. Shortly after that diagnosis, the vet changed his mind: the filly had been poisoned.

Trying to look back more than a century into a small barn in a little town in western Indiana is frustrating, and armchair diagnosis in the absence of an autopsy (or necropsy, in the case of a horse) is bad medicine even when the patient is right next door. Was Lady Patch poisoned? If she was, did Manley Sturges have anything to do with it?

On the pro-poison side, tetanus, while it killed most horses who contracted it in those pre-vaccine days, didn't kill within a matter of hours between the first symptoms and the death. What's more, tetanus symptoms—stiffness and spasm—usually aren't similar to those of poison. The initial diagnosis was clearly wrong.

On the pro-Sturges as villain side, he wanted Dan Patch and may have hoped to suggest in some twisted way that if he couldn't have him, he could hire someone to make sure that Dan Messner didn't either. He didn't have a reputation for violence, but he crossed paths with men who did.

On the other side, horses are capable of poisoning themselves. They have sensitive digestive systems, they cannot vomit, and many will eat anything within reach, including common pasture plants that are toxic to horses. A horse can eat something moldy or rotted or toxic, then develop colic and die within hours.

On the anti-Sturges as poisoner side, Dan Patch was not the only promising horse in the county that might be of interest to a man looking to step further over the line to the right side of the law. Hiring someone to poison a horse in a distant town in a stall next to the horse he coveted would have been a lot more work and much more dangerous than finding another object of desire.

If he was looking for fame—unlikely, given his inclination—a trotter would have been a better choice anyway. If he was looking for a profitable resale, Dan Patch's price was already high and one bad step on the track could reduce his value by thousands. Dan

Patch was no secret, and he was already past the point where he could bring profits in the betting ring or at resale.

Well after the fact, there was gossip in Oxford that the secretive New Yorker might have been sending a message. But there's no evidence now that much if any of the talk happened before the filly's death. What's more, nobody in little Oxford mentioned seeing a suspicious stranger in the area. On balance, it seems unlikely that Lady Patch was deliberately poisoned or that Manley Sturges had anything to do with it if she was. Unlikely, but not impossible.

But regardless of the cause of Lady Patch's death, it had one result. Dan Messner agreed to sell his horse to Manley Sturges. Myron McHenry negotiated the sale, for the same $20,000 offered the previous summer. McHenry, who had known Sturges since his days as James Butler's favorite race driver, had advised Messner against selling a few months earlier but had now changed his mind. It's possible that one of the Sturges offers came directly to McHenry and included a commission. It's likely that Sturges offered a better profit-sharing deal than Messner had. McHenry arrived in Oxford on March 18, 1902, to take Dan Patch away by train.

Dan Messner told reporters that he agreed to the sale for a number of reasons, including the record price, the highest ever paid for a pacer. He mentioned the demands of work from the store and other business, and then he talked about the things that all racehorse owners do when they lose or sell a great animal. He had a better one in the barn, he said, referring to Dan Patch's young half brother Messner. He pointed out that he still owned Zelica, the dam, and said "I think I can raise several Dan Patches."

Dan Messner would discover two things. It's not as easy to raise a great horse as it seems when you first do it, and the great ones are more than the sum of their parts. The fact is, you almost never do get another truly great one, no matter how hard you try and how many foals his dam produces. Dan Messner continued to own horses for years, most of them related to his one great horse, but he never had anything even vaguely resembling Dan Patch.

McHenry announced that Dan Patch would train over the admirable new track at Empire City, but he instead sent him to the Speedway stables of John J. Quinn, known as the Sycamore of Harlem for his height and importance. Quinn, a longtime stalwart of Tammany Hall and one of the most powerful figures in New York racing, was the superintendent of the Speedway.

Dan Patch's presence at the Quinn stable was probably Manley Sturges's doing. Sturges, Lichtenstein, and others in the high-end gambling business often drove side by side on the Speedway with wealthy friends and clients. Sturges in fact toyed with the notion of driving Dan Patch himself in the annual Speedway parade, scheduled for May 10, and may have made the purchase with the idea of showing off his new horse to the rich amateurs before getting down to the business of racing. He thought better of it and allowed McHenry to handle the reins for training miles in April.

By early May, Dan Patch was at Empire City Trotting Park in Yonkers in Charles Thompson's stable where he would continue preparations for the 1902 Grand Circuit season. Thompson was an old Illinois friend of McHenry's, and Sturges agreed on the move since Empire City owner James Butler was a business associate.

In late May, there was already evidence that Sturges and McHenry weren't exactly sure what to do with their horse. McHenry, perhaps feeling a little guilt over the loss of a heat in 1901, began a campaign to eliminate heat racing and to change the standard of harness competition to the dash, where each field competes in a single mile race. Shortly after this, he announced that he wanted a match race with Anaconda, the great pacer he had driven in 1899 and 1890. The race would consist of the best three heats of five.

Sturges, meanwhile, bought a new horse to be trained by McHenry: Freddie C., a horse with a respectable but not spectacular race record in the West. The two horses paced easy miles together at Empire City, with one newspaper reporter noting that Dan Patch "acts very anxious to cut loose" and Freddie C. "looks like a sure money earner." Freddie was soon renamed Prince Direct, a name better suited to a sure money earner.

Dan Patch, it seemed, wasn't going to be as easy to campaign as they thought, and they looked around for alternatives. McHenry moved his small string to Cleveland, where he had driven his first training mile with Dan Patch just over a year earlier. He got the word out that Dan had paced a one-eighth mile in thirteen seconds, an extraordinarily quick time.

McHenry and Sturges decided to mirror the previous year's campaign, beginning with Windsor, Ontario. Instead of a modest race, they agreed to a match with the Canadian pacer Harold H., whom Dan had defeated in Memphis. Harold was supposed to be much better in 1902, but that proved not to be the case and Dan Patch found himself an easy win in three quick heats. It was then on to Grosse Pointe for the opening of the Grand Circuit, then back to Cleveland. In each case, easy wins came in straight heats, although McHenry tried to make the first heat in Cleveland look closer than it was.

McHenry and Sturges were not getting what they wanted out of the season. They knew going in that Dan Patch was no longer a betting proposition. With purses in pacing races as modest as they were, there wasn't much money to be won on the racetrack either. Now, there was less publicity as well. Results of his races began to sink lower and lower in newspaper reports with the apparent inevitability of his victories. Whether Sturges bought the horse to resell him at a handsome profit, with McHenry in line for a commission—or if he acquired Dan Patch as part of a giant leap towards respectability—unnoticed perfection was proving unsatisfying.

On July 31 McHenry and Sturges announced that Dan Patch's next race would be against a horse who wouldn't be there. On August 2, the final day of the Grand Circuit meet at Columbus, Ohio, Dan Patch would attempt to better his sire Joe Patchen's record of 2:01¼. With that announcement, Dan Patch's competitive racing career was over and his name returned to the headlines.

The August 3 *Boston Globe* told the story in bold print. The headline: Great Dan Patch. The first subhead: Goes a Mile at Columbus in 2:00¾ With Ease. The second subhead: Son of Joe Patchen Fastest Pacer the Turf Has Ever Known. The *Globe* wasn't entirely accurate. Star Pointer still held the record of 1:59¼, but suddenly that mark seemed in great jeopardy.

With a running horse alongside to urge him on, Dan Patch had taken three-quarters of a second off Joe Patchen's record with apparent ease, and most observers believed he could have finished in less than two minutes if McHenry had asked him to do it. McHenry said afterwards that Dan Patch would pass Star Pointer before the end of the year.

The strategy of racing against time had worked. According to one newspaper report, the actual races of the day were "tame and uninteresting" and Dan Patch had his headlines back. He was rarely out of the news for the rest of the summer and fall of 1902.

Attention meant money. Managers of racetracks and representatives of racing organizations negotiated for Dan Patch's presence, hoping their fans might be the ones to witness the new world record. Myron McHenry conducted most of the negotiations, as Manley Sturges was oddly absent for most of the summer.

In January 1902 William Travers Jerome, the anti-gambling magistrate, had taken over as district attorney and all casino operators were scrambling to deal with the threat. This may also have been the time Sturges was negotiating the sale of the Victoria Club to Davey Johnson, a deal worth many times the offers coming in for Dan Patch appearances.

McHenry worked out an ambitious schedule of record-breaking attempts, with decidedly mixed results. High winds made a world record attempt impossible at Brighton Beach, but he managed another 2:00¾. At Readville, he inexplicably broke stride twice. On a third attempt, he took a quarter second off his personal best.

By August 29 Manley Sturges had his other business sufficiently under control to be on hand in Providence to see his horse pace a runner-prompted mile in 1:59½, just a quarter second off Star Pointer's world record. It was on to Philadelphia and Syracuse and Empire City. Each saw good miles and huge crowds. Then on September 23, back at the Readville track in Massachusetts, came a 1:59¼ mile. That tied Star Pointer's world record.

In four more exhibitions in October, at Cincinnati, Terre Haute, Davenport, and Memphis, Dan Patch failed to lower the record further, but he drew monstrous crowds and hundreds of headlines. By the end of the season, almost no horseman or fan in the country doubted that Dan Patch would stand alone at the top of the racing pyramid by the middle of the next year.

But by the following season Manley Sturges would no longer be standing next to him and Myron McHenry would be clinging precariously to his halter. Dan Patch had picked up an admirer during his 1902 season, one with both money and determination, much as Sturges had been a year previously. When the offers and counteroffers had worn themselves out, Manley Sturges was left without Dan Patch, but with a handsome profit and with a new and better reputation.

10

RACE AGAINST TIME

MARION WILLIS SAVAGE, known as Will, made his first offer for Dan Patch in a wire to Manley Sturges in mid-spring of 1902, well before the horse's first start of the year. How much he offered isn't known, but it was probably only slightly more than the $20,000 Sturges had just paid Dan Messner.

The deal wasn't accepted, and Savage said later that he was convinced that Sturges would sell at a reasonable price if Dan Patch failed to surpass Star Pointer's record during the rest of the racing season. Savage followed Dan off and on through the season, dressed so soberly that McHenry and his stable workers began calling him "The Parson." Some of them claimed they had no idea who the Parson was, but in reality Myron McHenry knew exactly who he was dealing with.

When Dan Patch finished the season only tied for the all-time record, Savage and Sturges, with McHenry as a go-between, opened negotiations. Why Sturges was ready to sell is unknown. The sale did give him a profit, although probably not as much as it would have if Dan had broken the record. Maybe he thought the record wasn't coming, in spite of Dan's relatively young age. It was unlikely that he needed money in December 1902, since he had plenty to invest in other enterprises. Perhaps the admiration that was being showered on the charismatic horse was attracting too much attention to a man who had always shrunk from publicity. Whichever was true, Manley Sturges wanted out.

Sturges and Savage came together at a figure of $60,000, by far the most ever paid for a pacer. Most of it was handed over in cash, but about $20,000 was believed to be the value of some other consideration. There's been speculation that Sturges accepted breeding rights, but he wasn't a breeder and no Dan Patch-sired foals ever appeared under his name.

Marion Willis Savage, maker of patent medicines and livestock feed, thought that he and Dan Patch together could become rich and famous. *(Photo: International Stock Food Farm Yearbook 1906)*

That is just about the only mysterious thing connected to Savage's ownership of Dan Patch. While Manley Sturges lived his life in the shadows, Will Savage lived his in the brightest ray of sunshine he could find. A century later he likely would have detailed every move in a website, explained every thought in a blog, and recorded every step on YouTube.

If Dan Messner was the quintessential small-town shopkeeper of the nineteenth century and Manley Sturges embodied the Gilded Age striver of flexible morality, Will Savage was the archetypal twentieth century American businessman. He was smart, ambitious, and eager to use the newest technology to advance himself and his business. He also liked to live well and wasn't reluctant to spend money he didn't have.

His story began as so many others have in this story, human and horse alike. He was born in a small town in the Midwest, in his case Stark County, Ohio, in the northeastern part of the state. His father, Edward Savage, trained to be a doctor and enlisted in the volunteer army when the Civil War broke out in 1861, leaving his wife and two-year-old Will in Ohio for the duration of the conflict.

After the war, the family moved to eastern Iowa. Rachel Savage had at one time been disowned by her Quaker family for marrying outside the faith. But when the Savages moved west they chose West Liberty in Muscatine County, where a number of Ohio Quakers had settled, including members of the controversial Hicksite sect to which some of Rachel's family belonged.

Dr. Savage farmed a little in West Liberty, practiced medicine in neighboring West Branch, and encouraged his son to go into medicine too. Will Savage did work for a while in a West Branch pharmacy but was more interested in farming, particularly in the breeding and training of horses. Later, after Savage became famous through Dan Patch, old-timers in West Branch remembered his devotion to his father's buggy horse, and his futile efforts to save her from a fatal case of colic.

This incident may have played a part in his eventual business career, but other circumstances of his growing up years started him down the path to his purchase of Dan Patch. Muscatine County was the perfect place to learn to love harness racehorses.

The first high-class trotting stallion was brought into the county in the early 1850s and well-bred mares soon followed. Young Will Savage joined many other county horsemen in his

Golden Bashaw, Savage's first harness racehorse, is idealized in a later drawing. *(Photo: International Stock Food Farm Yearbook 1906)*

admiration of a stallion named Green's Bashaw, also known as Bashaw 50, a representative of a line of trotting horses that was in the process of being eclipsed by the descendants of Hambletonian. Both he and his offspring were better looking than the Hambletonians, often gray or black with a splash of white, but they weren't quite as fast at the trot. Green's Bashaw lived on a neighboring farm near West Liberty from 1865 to 1876 and an eighteen-year-old Savage managed to acquire a great grandson he named Golden Bashaw.

By the time he was able to buy expensive racehorses, neither Savage nor anybody else would have intentionally picked a horse of the Bashaw line just because of its breeding. But as he studied the bloodlines of Dan Patch, he would have been pleased to discover six Bashaw horses, three on each side of the pedigree. He didn't know at the time that Green's Bashaw was among them, appearing only as "Bashaw Horse" as the sire of Joe Patchen's grandmother. But that discovery was in the future.

In 1881 the newly married Will Savage tried farming in central Iowa, but the failure of the farm and the death of Dr. Savage early in 1882 led to the establishment of the Dr. E. W. Savage Medicine Company in Iowa Falls in 1883. Dr. Savage was gone, but his name lived on in *Dr. Savage's Pulmonary Balsam, Stomach Regulator, May Apple Syrup*, and half a dozen other medicines. With the creation of the company, Will Savage became part of the massive American patent medicine industry.

At least a thousand different companies were involved in the manufacture of the inaccurately named patent medicines during the second half of the nineteenth century. The substances were not actually patented, since none of the manufacturers would reveal the contents. They were not as concerned that rivals would discover the properties of their special remedies as they claimed. What they did want was to prevent customers from knowing just how ordinary the contents were. So they trademarked the name of the remedy and the design of the label, and they copyrighted the increasingly elaborate art used in the advertising.

Americans spent millions of dollars each year on patent medicines for themselves and their animals, and Will Savage hoped to get some of that for himself. The remedies he produced were supposedly developed by the late Dr. Savage, whose name was on every bottle, but it's hard to know at this point if that was true. The company did well enough to move to larger quarters in Dubuque but was out of business by 1888, most likely because of a limited budget for advertising. That was not a mistake that Will Savage would repeat.

Savage was one of three important figures in Dan Patch's story who involved themselves in the patent medicine business. In the mid-1890s Myron McHenry lent his name to *McHenry's Leg and Body Liniment* "for the benefit of bicyclists, athletes, and horses." In the early 1900s Manley Sturges, probably looking for a place to park his money, started the Excelsior Manufacturing Company, near Washington Square in New York, for the purpose of making patent medicines. Neither McHenry nor Sturges succeeded in the business.

With the failure of Dr. Savage's Medicine Company, Will Savage moved his family and his ambition to Minneapolis where he revived his patent medicine business, adding human and veterinary remedies under the name Dr. Belden. A favorite was

Dr. Belden's Six Prairie Herbs. A federal regulator later reported, "the odor and taste suggested highly diluted and sweetened whiskey with a very small amount of some indifferent herbs." The company was fined ten dollars for false and fraudulent advertising. But *Six Prairie Herbs* and other remedies sold well, whether it was the whiskey or the "indifferent herbs" that did the trick.

The centerpiece of the new farm was a barn that looked like the Taj Mahal.
(Photo: International Stock Food Farm Yearbook 1906)

As Dr. Belden, who apparently didn't exist, searched for a market share, Savage changed the primary focus of his business. He was one of a thousand makers of elixirs for humans, but he would be among only a handful of makers of medicated feed supplements for animals. Feed itself would be difficult and expensive to transport long distances, but concentrated supplements, supposedly containing special nutrients, could be profitable. Thus was born the International Stock Food Company, whose waterfall of ads proclaimed "Three Feeds for One Cent" in the concoction of "roots, herbs, barks, and seeds." What bark and which seeds were never specified.

Both the remedies and the supplements were heavily advertised, even when Savage had to borrow money to create and

Savage purchased the Minnesota Exposition Building for his stock food business. (Drawing: International Stock Food Farm Yearbook 1906)

distribute printed material. He hired his own lithographers, started his own printing company, and created new products for man and animal. By the time he took possession of Dan Patch, he was employing 300 workers in his medicine and supplement company and dozens more on a luxurious farm he was building on 700-acres of bluff and bottom land on the banks of the Minnesota River south of Minneapolis. The main barn was to look remarkably like a wooden Taj Majal.

Savage was also in the middle of negotiations to buy the Minnesota Exposition Building, which would give International Stock Food workers 750,000 square feet of elbow room. He didn't really need such space, and still didn't after future expansions, but lithographs of the building must have caused a few jaws to drop among the farmers who received printed matter from International Stock Foods.

Savage's farm manager, Harry C. Hersey, suddenly found himself in charge of the county's most famous horse. (Photo: International Stock Food Farm Yearbook 1906)

He was a man who thought big and dreamed bigger. He wanted to own the best horse breeding operation in the world and he wanted the world's best horses grazing in its pastures. A year before his successful purchase of Dan Patch, Savage had taken the train to New York where, at Madison Square Garden, he bid $12,100 for Directum, once the champion trotting stallion although long since retired from the track. He added a $1300 successful bid for a yearling daughter of Directum, a lot of money for an untried young horse. The Garden, the last of the four buildings of the same name to actually be located at Madison Square, was a favorite site for high-end sales, as well as the circus, boxing, and musical performances it was famous for.

A few hours after his successful bid for Directum, Savage had reason to think that profit was inevitable in the breeding business. A group of men from California offered him $25,000 for his new stallion. He turned them down and shipped Directum to Minnesota.

Advising Savage on his first foray into big money horse buying was Harry Cook Hersey, his new farm trainer. The thirty-three-year-old Hersey had gone to work for Savage during the summer of 1901 expecting to be the manager of a breeding operation. Always a horseman, he had learned the farm business in western Indiana, not far south of Dan Patch's Oxford. He worked for Peter Kaufman of Terre Haute, a market breeder of both Thoroughbred and Standardbred horses. After leaving Indiana, Hersey worked briefly in Kentucky, preparing and selling horses.

Hersey came to Minnesota with knowledge of stallion management, broodmare care, and the preparation of horses for sale. What he didn't know a lot about was racing, and it was obvious to everybody that Dan Patch was too young and too fast to retire to farm life, no matter how well appointed the farm. Myron McHenry agreed to stay on as Dan's racetrack trainer and driver, but people who knew Will Savage suspected that it was just a matter of time before two difficult personalities collided.

Problems were still in the future on January 5, 1903, when Dan Patch arrived in Minneapolis in a specially fitted railroad car. Most of the racetrack people around the country had expected him to be stabled for the winter at a racing barn in Kansas City. He would be transferred to Minnesota for the breeding season in the spring. He'd then go to McHenry in May to his base at the Glenville track in Cleveland to be prepared for the racing season. Imagine their surprise when news got out that he was going immediately to Minneapolis, where he would winter in the city. Imagine McHenry's surprise too.

That's what happened after Dan was greeted by a couple of marching bands, speechmaking, and a march down Nicollett Avenue in front of several thousand cheering residents. He loved the attention, as he had learned to at the racetrack, and it turned out that he loved the urban lifestyle. Living in a comfortable stall in the stable behind Will Savage's city mansion, he enjoyed treats and visitors and regular jaunts pulling his new owner's family around in a sleigh. McHenry would have been horrified had he known.

He also enjoyed his spring work, running around in newly laid out paddocks at the International Stock Food Farm in Hamilton, about ten miles south. And he enjoyed being bred to about twenty mares for a $300 stud fee, although the price was negotiable. In the meantime, Savage got to work on his plans to make back his $60,000.

First, in late January, he announced that he had insured Dan Patch for $112,000. The figure was improbably high, since people a century ago usually insured only for the money they had invested in something, not for what they assumed it might be worth someday. But if Savage's goal wasn't so much to protect his financial investment, (which it wasn't), the insurance worked out just fine. His announcement prompted dozens of stories nationwide.

That led right into his second goal of the winter and spring. He began arranging appearances for Dan Patch—not races, and not even record attempts, exactly. He thought about sending Dan Patch on a tour of the Deep South, to give half the country its first look at him. He thought about the same tracks Dan had raced over the season before, the ones most likely to offer up a chance at Star Pointer's record. He even thought about displaying his star at horse shows.

What he wasn't inclined to think about was a matchup with the country's other active two minute pacer, a nine-year-old gelding named Prince Alert, who had reached the magical mark the previous October in Memphis, although with less publicity than Dan Patch received. What's more, Prince Alert had set the all-time record for a rarely used distance, a half-mile, at the same race meet.

Prince Alert had none of Dan Patch's charisma, neither staring at the spectators in the stands nor bowing to their cheers. His driver and trainer, Mart Demarest, although highly experienced, wasn't called the "wizard of the sulky" as Myron McHenry was. Prince Alert raced in hopples, rather than free-legged as Dan Patch did, which somehow made him less admirable. And he didn't have an owner like Will Savage, who could find publicity in an insurance bill.

Savage, who was already including Dan Patch in his ads for feed supplements, was not inclined to risk his horse's unique popularity with risky ventures, like entering a race he might lose, or going after a record he might not break. So he delayed sending Dan back to an increasingly nervous Myron McHenry. McHenry had given up the other three horses he was training for Manley Sturges, including two fast ones, in order to concentrate on Dan Patch for the 1903 season.

Dan finally arrived in June at McHenry's base at the Glenville track in Cleveland, along with a Boston terrier and a red and gold gamecock as mascots. His trainer's relief was mixed with worry that he had little time to prepare for a racing season—a season that would likely include competition with Price Alert, if not head to head, then stopwatch to stopwatch.

He may have been made a little more nervous on June 26 when the news broke that Walter Gentry of Bloomington, Indiana, had offered $92,000 for Dan Patch and Directum, an offer that had been rejected. Gentry owned a traveling circus and it seemed likely that Savage let the word out to show the world that his own plans for Dan Patch were far more noble than hauling him around as a circus attraction. McHenry wondered how many more offers were on the horizon.

So McHenry came up with an owner-pleasing idea. Instead of a race or a record-attempting mile, neither of which he was confident Dan could manage on short training, they would go after Prince Alert's half-mile record. He set a date of July 17 and a location at the fast mile track at Columbus, but he allowed journalists to believe that he and Dan would pace an exhibition mile with no promises made. They did that, in a quick but not record-setting time, and then McHenry announced that they would time-trial a challenge to Prince Alert's half-mile record.

After warming up in front of the grandstand they moved to the half-mile pole on the far side of the track and took off at full speed. In spite of strong headwinds in the stretch, Dan Patch equaled Prince Alert's half-mile record of 57¾ seconds. It was an extraordinary performance given the conditions. Dan seemed destined to lower his and Star Pointer's all-time mile record and to do it soon.

The time came at Brighton Beach in Brooklyn a month later, where Dan Patch had first attracted the attention of eastern money two years earlier. McHenry intended to go after sole possession of the all-time pacing record, but August 19 turned out cold, damp, and windy: three conditions that made success unlikely. After warming up, McHenry told starter Frank Walker that he would go after Dan's own track record of 2:00¼, rather than the faster time, so his performance would seem less of a failure.

McHenry used two galloping Thoroughbred prompters, one directly in front, to give his horse something to overcome. Dan Patch seemed to relish the challenge, although a third quarter slightly slower than the first two had some observers worried. They needn't have, as Dan pushed himself to a sub-thirty second final quarter, pacing out the mile in 1:59, by three quarters of a second the fastest mile under harness in history. Star Pointer was now in second place, and Dan looked for all the world like he could have gone faster. The crowd erupted and Dan Patch posed for the spectators on his way off the track.

A handful of doubters pointed out that the front-running Thoroughbred lessened the wind resistance but their voices were drowned out by the roar of thousands of thrilled spectators who thought it was no time for quibbling. Even the doubters suspected that Dan Patch, prompter or no prompter, would lower the record again during the season. He had broken the record in poor conditions and with no apparent distress. The Brighton Beach record wasn't going to be the end of the story.

But a funny thing happened on the way to the record. Rather than being paced into oblivion, Prince Alert stayed right in the public eye and no worse than even with Dan Patch in speed. Myron McHenry had seen it coming. He knew that Mart

Prince Alert made his record with the lead prompter carrying a sail-like windbreaker. (Photo: Munsey's Magazine October 1903)

Demarest felt Prince Alert was the fastest horse in training and had resented the attention showered on Dan Patch. The previous November in Memphis he had tried to prove it.

On October 31,1902, he had overheard McHenry ask to be put on the following day's card for a time trial and then requested a spot for Prince Alert as well. Each paced a mile individually, with Prince Alert going half a second faster. Demarest was determined that the rest of the racing world should recognize his horse's superiority.

On September 7, 1903, in Lima, Ohio, Dan Patch set a record on a half-mile track, because of the four turns to a mile always slower than a mile track, of 2:04. Less than a week later Prince Alert broke the record in Pennsylvania with a 2:03½ mark. But the worst news was yet to come. On September 23 Dan failed in his attempt to lower his 1:59 world record in Columbus, but his people were pleased that he went in 1:59½, still one of the fastest miles in history, third only to his own and Star Pointer's records. But the next day they got some bad news. At James Butler's magnificent mile at Empire City in Yonkers, Prince Alert paced an exhibition mile in 1:57, a full two second less than Dan Patch's month-old record.

At first McHenry and Savage couldn't believe it. Then they began to read details of the gelding's remarkable performance. The weather was perfect, with not a breath of air to be felt. The track was hard and fast, as good as the best track superintendent could make it. Demarest had taken himself out of the sulky, giving the drive to the smaller and lighter Jack Curry, but he drove the lead prompting horse himself. Most of all, and worst of all, Prince Alert was not only wearing the contemptible hopples to keep him at the pace, but the lead runner was carrying an extraordinary contrivance on his sulky.

Many time-trialers, including Dan Patch himself, had begun to race behind a modest dirt screen fixed to the seat of the lead horse's sulky. This was designed, its proponents claimed, merely to keep dirt out of the eyes of horse and driver. There was loud debate, however, as to whether it served to divert air and contribute a second or so to the time of the horse.

Nobody had any doubt about Prince Alert's new windshield, designed with the assistance of officials at Empire City who wanted a record for their own track. His time was a full two and a half seconds faster than his best-ever time, an improvement that just doesn't happen. The device was an extraordinary combination of sail and tent constructed on the back part of the sulky of the lead horse. Prince Alert's nose was kept directly behind the screen until the stretch. He paced most of the race in a frictionless vacuum.

"Foul!" cried Savage and McHenry.

"Nonsense!" replied Demarest. He added that McHenry could try to rig up something similar for himself as could any other trainer.

As it turned out, judges for the American Trotting Register eventually disallowed records made with the windshield, and Prince Alert's lifetime best returned to 1:59½. He never again approached a world record. But as far as anybody knew in September of 1903, Dan Patch was no longer world champion.

Since Dan Patch was long committed to a schedule, McHenry and Savage had to wait for a month for a real shot at regaining the record. It came at Memphis, where a year before Prince Alert's trainer had tried to prove that his horse was faster.

McHenry arrived with unusual confidence. The week before in Lexington, Kentucky, he had driven Dan Patch to a world record pulling a wagon. The awkward and much heavier wagon was rarely used in competition, but the record existed and Will Savage had wanted to recover a little of Dan's lost luster.

They couldn't have expected how much glitter was to be regained. He crossed the finish line in 1:59½, two and a half seconds faster than the previous world record for the wagon and just half a second slower than his own best sulky mile. Still, odds in the betting rings were against his breaking the world record. Prince Alert's time was just too fast, too impossible, especially since Dan Patch would not be racing behind a windshield.

McHenry did rig the lead prompter with a small canvas strip between the wheels to limit dirt kickback, and put two following prompters on the track. With four quarter miles of almost exactly twenty-nine seconds each, Dan Patch thundered across the finish line in 1:56¼, three-quarters of a second faster than the hoppled, shielded Prince Alert. The Memphis crowd erupted and Myron McHenry threw his hat into the air.

Prince Alert's people tried desperately to get their record back. The next day in Providence, the gelding took a quarter second from Dan Patch's world record for a half mile and his owners demanded a match race. The demand was answered by both silence and action. The match race was not accepted and five days later, still at Memphis, Dan Patch responded by taking a full second and a half off Prince Alert's new half-mile record.

He followed forty-five minutes later with a world record mile for the wagon, two seconds faster than he had paced at Lexington.

There were two more stops on Dan Patch's 1903 schedule, visits to Alabama and Georgia, where he and McHenry acquired the remaining world records: one for the high-wheeled sulky and another for the two-mile distance. In reality, though, three things ended in Memphis: Dan Patch's competitive season, his rivalry with Prince Alert, and his relationship with Myron McHenry. In Memphis, McHenry let the word out that he and Will Savage were parting company. He didn't say why.

11

FAME AND FORTUNE

THE DEPARTURE OF Myron McHenry marked the end of Dan Patch's career as a racehorse and the beginning of his life as a full-time celebrity. To be sure, he hadn't actually raced for nearly a year and a half, but with McHenry at the reins there was always the chance that he might again compete with something other than a stopwatch. Will Savage saw no races in his great horse's future, none at all, since they threatened too much to lose from a defeat and too little to win from a victory.

Savage made no secret of what he was planning, and McHenry himself claimed that the primary reason for the split was his opposition to the idea of Dan Patch being "circused" around the country. There were other reasons, to be sure, including—according to Savage—McHenry's drinking and—according to McHenry—Savage's second-guessing of McHenry's training decisions.

Other horses had been used in time trials, and other horses had traveled around the country to do it, but none had left competition for exhibition in the prime of their careers. Nor had it been seen in other sports, where stars didn't tour as celebrities until it was clear they could no longer win, and Savage faced industry-wide grumbling when it became obvious that he was going to do it to harness racing's all-time champion. He responded that Dan Patch would still try to lower his own records, but he would do it in front of people who didn't normally see the big time racing of the Grand Circuit.

It shouldn't have come as a surprise. Will Savage had been producing patent medicines for over twenty years and was now most famous for a medicine-like livestock feed supplement. His ads were already suggesting that his feed was responsible for Dan Patch's improbably fast miles the previous year. An exhibition season would be like a huge medicine show, in the tradition of the traveling shows that offered small towns a little entertainment, a little information, and a lot of hope that a bottle of a secret remedy would cure whatever was wrong. Plenty of bottles would be sold if the show were good enough, just like plenty of bags of horse feed supplement were shipping out of the International Stock Food headquarters every day.

But Savage had a more fitting model for Dan Patch's new career. For twenty years, Buffalo Bill Cody had been touring the country in his popular Wild West show, drawing hundreds of thousands of spectators over the course of a season, selling thousands of dollars worth of tickets, and making even more money selling his dime novels.

Buffalo Bill Cody provided a prototype for a lucrative, publicity-driven career. (Photo: Library of Congress)

Like Dan Patch, Buffalo Bill hadn't entirely left his real career, in his case as a frontier scout. In 1876 he put a theatrical season on hiatus as he went west to help chase Sitting Bull after Custer's defeat at the Little Big Horn. In 1890 he was back west to negotiate with Sitting Bull, by now his friend and former employee in the Wild West show, who was showing signs of joining an Indian rebellion in South Dakota.

But the show remained the focus of Cody's life as well as the source of his fame and considerable income. He was skilled at scheduling, transportation, negotiating contracts, and spotting talent—all of which contributed to the success of the Wild West Show. But two things were most important to Buffalo Bill's preeminence: he provided a consistently good show and he promoted and advertised it relentlessly. Will Savage would do the same with Dan Patch. He booked his great horse in nearly a dozen cities and began planning his advertising campaign.

Savage ordered a specially decorated railroad car to transport the champion over what he estimated would be 10,000 miles of rail during 1904 alone. The car was palatial, with half designated as a private stall for Dan Patch and the rest as accommodations for the prompting horses and grooms. The white car featured huge paintings of Dan on each side, M. W. Savage's name in

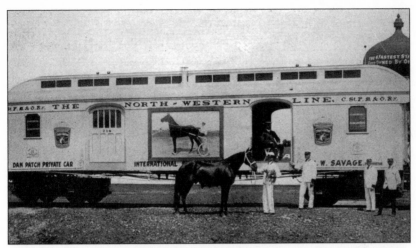

Dan Patch's custom railroad car allowed him to be transported in great luxury and provided a rolling advertisement. *(Photo: International Stock Food Farm Yearbook 1906)*

large letters, and appropriately generous ads for International Stock Foods. If that car came through a town too little to merit a stop, the people of the town would enjoy and remember the sight anyway. Walt Disney's Fulton Corners in *So Dear to My Heart* was such a town.

In the meantime, there was money to be made in the breeding shed. Over the winter, Savage had acquired several new brood-mares, including Maude, the dam of Martha Marshall, the only horse to beat Dan Patch in a heat in a Grand Circuit race. Savage hoped that the lure of Dan Patch would have owners shipping their mares in from Kentucky and Indiana and New York in spite of the distance and the cold weather, but if they didn't, he had plenty of mares himself. The home mares, plus several whose owners paid a stud fee of as much as $500, made up what Savage announced as a book of fifty-seven mares for the 1904 breeding season. If true, it was a huge number in those pre-artificial insemination days.

Whether it was too much time in the breeding shed, or training miles that weren't quite challenging enough, or Harry Hersey's inexperience on real racetracks, or maybe it was the quality of the racing surfaces, but Dan Patch failed to impress in his first exhibition appearances of 1904. His seasonal debut was scheduled for August 11 in Indianapolis, and a carload of Oxford, Indiana, men traveled to see him, including old John Wattles. Heavy rain damaged the track, though, and the Oxford men had to be satisfied with a stable visit. They claimed Dan recognized them and they were certainly pleased to see him again.

They would not have been so pleased had they stayed for the next day, when Dan Patch paced his slowest mile in two years on a full mile track, although the muddy surface drew most of the criticism. Two weeks later in Des Moines, he failed to lower his own record for a half-mile track, even breaking stride. The next week, in Lincoln, Nebraska, came another comparatively slow mile, even though it was a state and track record. On September 6 at the Wisconsin State Fair, Dan Patch's mile was a little better, but world records still seemed far in the past and farther in the future. He was by now eight years old, not old by the standard of 1904 but possibly, reporters speculated, old enough to be showing the wear and tear of an ambitious racing career.

But an unexpected thing was happening at these appearances. Only Will Savage and Harry Hersey appeared to be disappointed with the times. The crowds were enormous, far larger than they normally were for racing events at the tracks. Forty thousand people in Des Moines and 50,000 in Milwaukee went home thrilled for just having laid eyes on the celebrated horse.

With no answer as to why the times were ordinary, it was on to Topeka for the Kansas State Fair in the elegant white railroad car. But almost immediately disaster struck. It was a calamity that turned out to be the worst thing that ever happened to the beautiful brown horse, but perhaps the best thing for his ambitious owner.

A few hours after being led off his special car in Topeka, Dan Patch began to show signs that something was very wrong. He was sluggish and uncooperative in a public workout, later developing a high fever and rapid heartbeat. When he showed signs of a distended belly, Harry Hersey and his grooms knew immediately that they were dealing with colic, then and now the leading killer of horses.

The fair's veterinarian and a distinguished veterinary surgeon called in from Kansas City diagnosed strangulated hernia, which, in 1904, was almost invariably fatal. In this condition, a section of intestine protrudes into the inguinal canal of the abdomen. If circulation to that section is cut off, it develops gangrene, infects, and kills the horse.

It was terrible news for Dan Patch and his people. Colic is a term that covers any kind of equine bellyache, ranging from an uncomfortable but minor case of gas to potentially fatal intestinal torsions. An infected inguinal hernia is and was just about the worst kind. Today, expensive and dangerous surgery can sometimes save a victim, but abdominal surgery was rarely performed on horses in 1904.

So as Dan Patch lay agonizing in his stall in Topeka, becoming increasingly feverish and with a weakening pulse, Hersey sent two wires to Minnesota—one to Will Savage and the other to the *Minneapolis Journal.* It's not known what he said to Savage, but he told the reporter that Dan Patch was going to die.

Savage wired more veterinarians to head to Topeka, and he jumped aboard a train to Kansas himself. As he traveled, word spread around the country of the champion's illness.

"Dan Patch will probably die," said the Lowell, Massachusetts, *Sun.* "Dan Patch will not live," declared the Racine, Wisconsin, *Journal.* "Dan Patch is at the point of death tonight," reported the *Nevada State Journal* of Reno. "Dan Patch likely to die," announced the *Washington Post.*

Before Savage arrived in Topeka, there was slightly better news. Dan's condition hadn't improved much, but one of the distinguished veterinarians who had been called in announced that the original diagnosis was incorrect. What Dan was suffering, he said, was impaction of the bowel, a blockage of the intestine usually caused by the ingestion of sand or chaff. That might be fatal, but equally it might pass.

The stories changed. "Dan Patch may yet recover," said the Sandusky, Ohio *Star.* The Eau Claire, Wisconsin *Telegram* reported that "Dan Patch is improved." Then, the Winnipeg *Star* told its readers, "Dan Patch has passed the critical stage and will doubtless recover," and the Pella,

Although Harry Hersey was the trainer and driver, most decisions were made by Will Savage. *(Photo: International Stock Food Farm Yearbook 1906)*

Iowa *Chronicle* reported on September 29, "Dan Patch alive and well."

He did survive, of course, but how he was saved and what really ailed him remains a mystery a century later. It is known that Will Savage arrived at Dan's stall at the Kansas State Fairgrounds late in the evening of September 13, carrying a bottle of International Colic Cure in his pocket. He went inside, spent the night with his horse, and in the morning Dan Patch was much better. Later, the story got out that Savage administered the remedy, thereby curing his dearly loved horse.

Savage himself never claimed that his colic remedy was responsible, but he did maintain that that triple doses of the International Stock Feed supplement over the next three weeks speeded Dan's recovery. Skeptics whispered that the supplement itself might have contributed to the impaction in the first place, if an impaction did actually take place. Other whisperers, even more skeptical, wondered if Dan Patch really ever had colic, pointing out that the incident got man and horse into literally hundreds of newspapers, making Dan even more of a beloved national figure than he had been before.

He almost certainly was ill, since Harry Hersey was always known to be an honorable man, even if a little overwhelmed by Will Savage's personality. But from the hindsight of a hundred years, it does appear that the first diagnosis, strangulated hernia, may have been what really ailed Dan. The horse's reported symptoms fit exactly with that diagnosis, and Dan Patch was a likely candidate. Adult victims are usually stallions, hard used in the stud (those fifty-seven mares in the spring qualify as hard use) or in active training for racing. Some studies show at least half of the victims are Standardbreds.

So how did Dan Patch survive this then-fatal disease? There is the occasional spontaneous resolution of the hernia. He just got better on his own.

Regardless of the specific disease or how it was cured, a weakened Dan, after a slow and careful appearance in front of Topeka spectators, was loaded back on the white car and transported to the International Stock Food Farm for further recuperation. The recovery period was short—shorter than most horsemen would have approved. On October 7 Dan Patch fulfilled a long-term obligation for an appearance at the Illinois State Fair in Springfield.

His time wasn't impressive, but the crowd was. More than 50,000 people were delighted to see the horse that newspapers were now referring to as the "national pet" looking healthy and very much alive. Two weeks after that, just over five weeks since being described as "dying," Dan Patch was back on the fast North Memphis Driving Park track to be part of a two week meet that was scoring headlines even before it started.

But the headlines rarely mentioned Dan Patch. Once he was safely healthy again, journalists lost interest in him. The big story in October 1904 was the competition between the big gelding Major Delmar and the little mare Lou Dillon for the trotting world record. The competition seemed destined to be settled at the Memphis meet after a season of trading records and one-upping each other in the size of the windshields they trotted behind.

As it turned out, the competition was entirely uncompetitive. Lou Dillon appeared terribly distressed and was badly beaten in the first of three heats. She raced well for half of the second heat before suddenly stopping, thereby losing the race. Years later, Major Delmar's trainer claimed he fed Lou Dillon a bottle of champagne before the race, causing her distress. How he could do this unnoticed and how a single bottle of champagne could cause such misery to a thousand pound horse were never explained.

On October 24 Dan Patch was sent to the track with just one runner alongside in an effort to break his and Star Pointer's unprompted record. Manley Sturges, who was on hand to see the attempt, was shocked at the sight of the horse he used to own.

"I felt so sorry for him," Sturges said afterwards. "He looked dull and weak, no more fit to wrestle with Star Pointer than a yearling would be."

Part of Dan Patch's appeal, shown here driven by Harry Hersey, were his exceptional good looks, which soon returned after his 1904 illness. (Photo: International Stock Food Farm Yearbook 1906)

Dan failed in his effort, pacing the mile in 2:00¼, earning only a paragraph in most papers. But close observers noted that this was the fastest mile of the year by any pacer. Manley Sturges said he thought that if Myron McHenry had been in the sulky, they would have broken the record.

Two days later, on October 25, the front-running prompter was back, and Dan Patch was sent out onto the Memphis track to go as fast as he could, which turned out to be fast indeed. It was, according to the *Washington Post*, "the fastest mile ever made by a horse in harness." The time of 1:56 took a quarter second off his own record and Dan was back in the headlines. To be sure, there was a little grumbling in the accompanying articles, pointing out that the three prompting runners placed Dan in a protected pocket for almost the entire mile.

Will Savage was quick to respond that the runners weren't around so much to help the pace as to please the fans, giving them a semblance of an actual race. Only fans were likely to accept that explanation, but the fact remained that Dan Patch had paced a mile in 1:56 and even purists had to acknowledge that no harness horse had ever gone so fast.

With that record to cap the season, plus the fact that Dan was still thin from his near-death experience less than two months earlier, he had surely earned a trip back home. He didn't get it. Savage had arranged for appearances at St. Louis, Oklahoma City, and Dallas.

All three tracks were in poor condition, but the one in Oklahoma City was dreadful, so deep and sandy that even a running horse would have trouble negotiating it. Hersey fitted a modest dirt shield to protect Dan from the sand kicked up by the lead

Savage himself often drove Dan Patch to sleigh in Minneapolis winters.
(Photo: International Stock Food Farm Yearbook 1906)

runner. A cloud of dust obscured the first three quarters, and as he approached the final quarter, Dan Patch hit an even deeper part of the track and briefly broke stride. Hersey and the horse's own athleticism prevented a fall.

In spite of the near fall, Dan Patch completed the mile. The time was stunning. He took a quarter second off his own world record for a half-mile track, one that resembled a beach more than a racing surface.

"Canes, hats, and coats filled the air," said one reporter, when the time of 2:03 was announced.

"It was the most wonderful mile ever paced by a horse," said Hersey. Although the 1904 season ended with a couple of high—very high—notes, a cloud of uneasiness hung over Dan and his crew.

Dan Patch was about to turn nine. Even a century ago, when horses usually had longer racing careers, most horses were well past their peak at nine. At such an age, improvement wasn't likely. There wasn't much left to adjust in the way of equipment, and the horse was well past the age of settling down. On the other hand, tendons and joints and hooves wear out, and being asked for speed and more speed on increasingly poor tracks wears them out even faster.

Will Savage apparently never considered retiring Dan Patch from his barnstorming career. Over the winter of 1904–1905, as Dan relaxed, first in Minneapolis pulling the family in a sleigh and then at the International Stock Food Farm, Savage scheduled more than a dozen appearances for his horse during 1905.

Dan served an entire stud season. He began full training only in June, and Savage scheduled him to appear at the Minnesota State Fair the first week in September.

The modern horseman would be appalled at this schedule. He wouldn't be campaigning a nine-year-old stallion anyway, and certainly not one with a full stud career underway. But along with contracting Dan Patch for exhibition and time trial appearances, Savage worked on promoting what was becoming a moneymaking machine on legs.

He issued a new advertisement for hundreds of newspapers and magazines in farm country, offering a new, free full-color print of Dan. You only had to give information on the livestock you owned and the publication where you saw the ad. Savage's

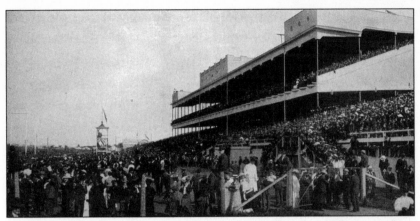

More than 98,000 people showed up on September 5, 1905, to see Dan Patch appear at the Minnesota State Fair. *(Photo: International Stock Food Farm Yearbook 1906)*

mailing list swelled. He offered a new "Dan Patch Two-Step" for fifty cents, or free with the purchase of a bag of International Stock Feed. And that wasn't all: The trickle of Dan Patch-related memorabilia and branded items was becoming a waterfall.

In July, Dan Patch offspring began appearing in number on Midwest racetracks. Ed Patch broke the track record winning a $1,000 stake at a small fairgrounds race meet at Monticello, Illinois. The time wasn't especially fast by his sire's standards, but the record 5,000 fans that crowded the stands looked familiar. An Iowa horseman bragged that his unraced Dan Patch colt, which he had named Robert Patch, ought to be considered the fastest colt in the world by inheritance.

In August, Hersey and Savage felt Dan was training well enough to invite reporters to witness a mile workout at the Minnesota State Fairgrounds, scheduled to be the site of his debit in September. On August 3, Dan Patch completed an effortless mile in 2:04, not quite time trial speed but more than respectable. He finished the last quarter without a prompter, without urging, and with Hersey's signal to take it easy with loose reins. His people began to have high hopes for the season.

Savage, wanted two things out of the season (not including substantial appearance money and increased sales of horse feed supplements): breaking his own, all-time fastest mile record of 1:56 and breaking Star Pointer's still-existing record for an unprompted mile of 1:59¼. Although the now nine-year-old Dan Patch had equaled that time two years earlier, Myron McHenry had used a front-running prompter for the first three-quarters.

He made six efforts in September, at fairs in Minnesota, Indiana, and Allentown Pennsylvania, plus an appearance in

Dan Patch warms up for his record-breaking mile in Lexington, Kentucky, October 7, 1905. *(Photo: International Stock Food Farm Yearbook 1906)*

Chicago. The times were good, but what left observers open mouthed was the size of the crowds. In Minnesota, the fair drew over 98,000 total admissions for the opening day appearance.

In Indianapolis 55,000 people showed up. Then in Allentown, more than 100,000 fans paid their admissions. Savage was pleased, since the arrangements at most of the venues called for him to receive a percentage of the admission money. He'd earned it, having peppered local newspapers with Dan Patch ads, supplied local feed dealers with piles of *Dan Patch Two-Steps,* and sent out thousands of full-color Dan Patch lithographs.

In early October, Dan shipped to Lexington, Kentucky, for what Will Savage believed was the most important meet at the fastest track in the country in front of the most knowledgeable fans. This, he decided, was where Dan Patch would set the records that would last forever and he was going to do everything he could to make it possible.

The year before, on a dusty track in Oklahoma City, Dan Patch had paced a magnificent mile with a modestly sized dust shield fastened to the back of the lead runner's sulky. As much as Will Savage might insist that the shield was designed only to prevent dirt from being thrown in Dan's face, he and Hersey knew that any horse would go a little faster with the wind broken by the contrivance. In Lexington, they worked out a device, carefully called a dirt shield (rather than windshield), that would protect from both wind and dirt. They insisted that it was different than the screen used by Prince Alert in his 1:57 mile two years earlier.

It was different in that it wasn't particularly effective, at least for reducing dust and dirt. On October 5, Dan Patch paced a mile behind his prompter in a cloud of dust, earning the title of "Black Whirlwind" from *the New York Times*. He tied his all-time record of 1:56 to the joy of the near-record crowd of 10,000. It was the fastest mile ever raced over the Lexington track.

The crowd was thrilled but Will Savage was not. He already had a horse who could go in 1:56. So, two days later, Dan Patch was back on the track in front of another crowd of ten thousand. The weather was perfect, warm with no wind, and Dan Patch was as sound and healthy as he had ever been. It was now or never, Savage and Hersey thought.

It turned out to be now. In front of an enthusiastic and knowledgeable crowd, Dan Patch and two running prompters took to the track just after four o'clock in the afternoon. At the start, the lead prompter, driven by the handsome young Scott Hudson, swerved a little, slowing Dan a fraction. The rest of the mile was smooth and easy, so easy that most fans thought they weren't seeing anything special. But when the judges posted the three-quarters time of 1:26¼ everybody knew what was happening.

Thousands of voices rose to urge Hersey, urge the prompters, and urge Dan Patch to greater speed. The noise rose and then nearly stopped as the horses flashed across the finish line and then rose to a roar even before the stewards posted the time. At the sight of the time—1:55¼—hundreds of fans broke through a police line to surround the horse, petting and touching him. His time was to remain a record for more than thirty years.

Dan Patch was unimpressed, wanting nothing more than to have his check rein removed so that he could stretch his neck. His calm was nearly as impressive as his time.

"He finished the mile as he had begun it," the previously skeptical *Boston Globe* reported. "He had scarcely broken a sweat."

After the record mile, Savage may or may not have received a huge offer for Dan Patch and it may or may not have been from Manley Sturges, who had been following the horse ever since selling him to Savage three years earlier. Savage announced to the press an offer made by "a syndicate of Easterners" immediately after the race, an offer that he quickly turned down. Savage was known to exaggerate, alter, and completely make up stories to reporters, and some historians think such an offer was never made. True or not, the story garnered another round of newspaper stories.

On the other hand, Harry Hersey said years later that Manley Sturges came up to him after the exhibition and asked him to wire an offer of $180,000 to Savage, which Savage quickly turned down. Hersey reported the offer nearly twenty years later, long after he had left Savage's emploment, and well after both Savage and Sturges were dead. Hersey was not known to exaggerate, alter, or make up stories. Yet he wouldn't have had to wire an offer, since Savage was right in Lexington and Sturges could have made the offer directly. At this point, the truth of the extraordinary offer is not likely to be known.

What was true was Savage's other post-record announcement—that Dan Patch would challenge Star Pointer's unprompted mile record, a mark that had been recently equaled by a pacer named Audubon Boy on the Lexington track. This so-called "in the open" record had become especially important, since there remained a few—although fewer, after the week in Lexington—who questioned Dan Patch's claim to be the fastest pacer ever. The dirt shield might not quite be as large as a windshield, but a lot of people presumed that it also took a second or so off a horse's time.

On October 13 Hersey again drove Dan Patch onto the Lexington racetrack, this time to go after the unprompted mile record. Strictly speaking, he was not unprompted. He began with a prompter alongside and a second running prompter joined the other at the top of the stretch. Neither raced in front, and no dirt or windshield was attached to either sulky. But the fresh prompter didn't help. A tired Dan Patch finished in 1:59¼, tying the mark for the second time. Savage himself claimed that his stopwatch showed 1:59, but only the official timers' results counted and there was no new record.

Although disappointed in the result, Savage wasn't planning to advertise the time even if his horse had gone a little faster. He had already ordered new ads and new lithographs titled "Dan Patch 1:55¼" and was beginning to distribute them. Although there was another month in the 1905 season, Savage decided against trying to lower the prompted record further, choosing to make one last furious assault on Star Pointer's unprompted record, which would inevitably be a little slower.

He would do it at Memphis, on a track that Dan Patch liked, in front of newspapermen and lovers of harness racing who would get the word out. On November 1, he and Hersey negotiated the mile in 2:00. On November 3 it was another record-tying 1:59¼ and on November 8 Savage insisted he try again. This time the mile went in 2:00. All performances were good. None was a new record but all were worth bragging about to Will Savage.

Savage, who appeared ready to stay in Memphis all winter if necessary, wanted to try again. On Saturday, November 11, he got perfect weather, warm and windless, and the record was his. The unprompted mile in 1:58 took more than a second off the record he had shared with Star Pointer and Audubon Boy. Dan Patch was the fastest harness racehorse in history, alone at the top of the mountain.

The Fastest Harness Horse
The World Has Ever Seen.

Dan Patch has eaten "International Stock Food" every day since 1902. Within 3 years after commencing to eat it he broke 12 world records. "International Stock Food" will give your horses more speed, strength and endurance.

250,000 People at 4 Exhibitions.

Dan Patch has paced 36 miles in 2:01½ to 1:55¼ and has paced 9 miles that averaged 1:57½. Dan paced 6 miles in 1905 that averaged 1:58. Within 30 days in the fall of 1905 Dan Drew 250,000 people in 4 exhibitions. This Tremendous Attendance of 250,000 people for four exhibitions has never been equalled or even approached in all harness horse history. Dan Patch broke 4 World Records and the Canadian half-mile track record, traveled 6000 miles in 66 days and finished the season strong, vigorous and absolutely sound.

The Greatest Exhibition Record Ever Made By a Harness Horse.

Exhibition Miles Paced By Dan Patch in 66 Days Commencing in Sept. 1905.

1st Mile	- -	1:59½
2nd Mile	- -	1:57½
3rd Mile, unpaced	-	2:00½
4th Mile, half-mile track	2:01
5th Mile, half-mile track to wagon	-	2:05
6th Mile, half-mile track	2:01½
7th Mile	- -	1:56
8th Mile -	-	1:55¼
9th Mile, unpaced	-	1:59¼
10th Mile, ½ mile track at Toronto, cold, track heavy	2:06
11th Mile, unpaced	-	2:00
12th Mile, unpaced	-	1:59¼
13th Mile, unpaced	-	2:00
14th Mile, unpaced		1:58

DAN PATCH EATS
3 FEEDS FOR ONE CENT.

BEAUTIFUL LITHOGRAPH FREE. A handsome six color lithograph of the world famous pacing champion, Dan Patch 1:55¼, mailed free, postage paid, if you state how many horses you own or care for. It is very life-like and an exact illustration of Dan pacing at his fastest clip.

INTERNATIONAL STOCK FOOD CO., MINNEAPOLIS, MINN., U. S. A.

This ad, printed in dozens of newspapers around the country, sums up Dan Patch's 1905 season, one of the most remarkable in racing history.

12

FINISH LINE

THE REST IS epilogue, at least in terms of Dan Patch's public career. He was never again as consistently fast as he was in the fall of 1905. In September 1906 he did pace a mile in 1:55 at the Minnesota State Fair, but the record was disallowed, as Will Savage knew it would be. The National Trotting Association, the organization that recognized records, ruled against it because of the use of the leading prompter and the dirt shield. The Lexington record was allowed to stand, however, and the great horse was officially known as "Dan Patch 1:55¼." So he is today.

Savage chose to use the figure 1:55 in his promotions and advertising anyway, and he occasionally claimed that Dan was about to go even faster. That possibility grew increasingly faint, although he remained consistently faster than most other horses in training until he was retired from timed performances after the 1909 season. By then, even the most ardent of Dan's admirers were ready to see him go. He had suffered his first lameness late in 1907 and had never been entirely sound since.

During his final season of touring he was joined by Minor Heir, a promising young pacer whom Savage hoped would revive flagging interest in his lame old champion. Improbable and unlikely victories by Dan Patch in head-to-head exhibitions with the energetic young Minor Heir seemed patently fake and distressed the people who loved and admired Dan, including, presumably, Will Savage. In December 1909 the almost fourteen-year-old Dan Patch was shipped home to Minnesota. He toured with the other horses the following year, but he never again performed at speed in front of a crowd.

Although his performing career was over, his advertising career continued without a hitch. He still made occasional public appearances, but they were limited to nearby events, including standing in a special tent on opening day of the Minnesota State Fair in 1911. His image continued to be spread around farm country as it had been since just a few weeks after Will Savage bought him from Manley Sturges.

Almost every significant event in Dan Patch's public life had been marked by a new magazine and newspaper ad, serving to keep his name before the public and assure that enormous crowds would come out to see him. The ads also served two other purposes. They usually publicized Savage products, not necessarily those related to horses, and they allowed Savage to continue compiling a mailing list that he eventually claimed included more than two million names.

Even if it wasn't quite as big as that, the list was prodigious. Savage managed to assemble it by offering readers something other than just an appeal to buy a product. He sent charts and animal care guides and offered entries in sweepstakes and, most important of all, he promised full color lithographs of Dan Patch. It didn't matter if the ad was for hog feed. He still offered the Dan Patch pictures.

Even better, Savage decided, were products actually bearing Dan Patch's name. Those would appeal to people who didn't own livestock but did admire his horse, opening up a new and even larger market. Some products Savage made or contracted for and sold out of his Minneapolis headquarters. With others, he licensed the name and the products were sold by unrelated companies.

Dan Patch was the first American athlete to endorse products on a significant scale. Early in 1903 Savage created the Dan Patch Music Company and produced the "Dan Patch March." In sheet music form, it was an important giveaway during the years of the quest for the mile record. Later that same year, he licensed the name to the Henschel Manufacturing Company of Milwaukee for the Dan Patch five-cent cigar. Human athletes didn't begin to catch up for a couple of years.

The best known of the first humans to be endorsed was shortstop Honus Wagner of the Pittsburgh Pirates, who is usually credited with being the first professional athlete to put his name on unrelated products. On September 1, 1905, Wagner signed a contract to endorse a series of Louisville Slugger baseball bats. He then appeared in ads for cigars, chewing gum, razor blades, and other products, taking payments for the endorsements.

Savage retained the use of Dan Patch's name for most of the farm related products and advertised them heavily in the Midwest and rural New England. The Dan Patch Spreader was a high-price and high-profit item, since farmers still mostly used their own animals' manure for fertilizer. The Dan Patch Gasoline Engine, as well as one bearing the name of Dan's son Dazzle Patch, was a big seller in farm country. The Dan Patch Washer, which included a big supply of Dan Patch Soap, sold throughout rural America.

Children's items, such as the Dan Patch Car and Dan Patch Racer, were popular, as were at least five versions of Dan Patch Cigars for their fathers. Dan Patch Gloves and Mittens were sold, as were scarves, stopwatches, thermometers, padlocks, and loose tobacco.

Honus Wagner of the Pittsburgh Pirates was a year behind Dan Patch in the endorsement competition. *(Photo: Library of Congress)*

Savage continued to offer books and lithographs of Dan Patch in connection with most of these items, and in 1909 offered a chance to win Forest Patch by counting the hairs on his body. He described Forest Patch as a $5,000 stallion, a three-year-old sired by Dan Patch. To participate, you had only to send for Savage's brand new Dan Patch lithograph. In exchange, Savage got names for his mailing list and presumably

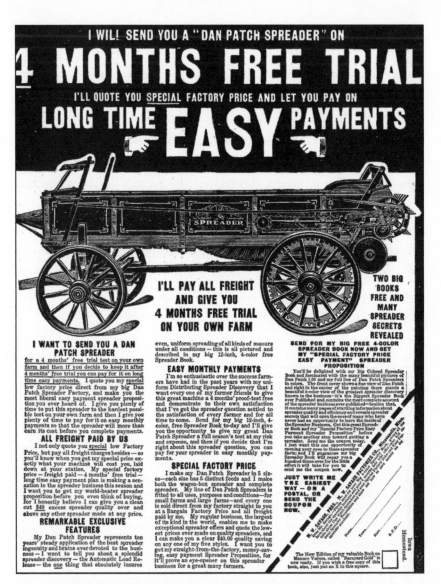

The Dan Patch Spreader proved a big success in farm country and was heavily advertised throughout the Midwest and New England.

got rid of a not very promising Dan Patch colt who wasn't worth anywhere near $5,000.

In fact, Dan Patch and the rest of the Savage breeding stock were worth less and less, as were everybody else's racehorses. The passage of the Hart-Agnew Law in New York in 1908 prohibited betting at racetracks and strengthened laws against off-track betting. The increasingly strict enforcement of the law, as well as new laws in other states, devastated the racing industry around the country over the next few years. Harness racing, with its focus in the Midwest, suffered less than Thoroughbred racing, which saw many of its great tracks close in 1911, but racehorse breeding of any kind was hardly a growth industry. Reformers then focused more of their attention on alcohol, and horse racing snuck back into normal operation.

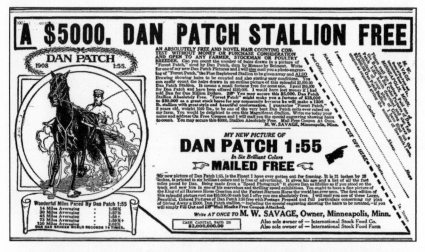

A chance to win the Dan Patch colt Forest Patch even showed up in some big city newspapers, but most of the people guessing the number of hairs on his body were in farm country.

The Dan Patch Line railroad was largely financed through Savage's relentless advertising, but it proved a financial drain on the International Stock Food Company.

Dan Patch was proving to be a respectable if not spectacular stallion. But the combination of his distance from breeding centers and the fact that so much was expected of him led to an inaccurate perception that he was a failure at stud. His offspring were good, not great, and that was a disappointment. However, his name remained golden.

In 1907 Will Savage decided to go into the railroad business and, as with almost everything else in their lives, the railroad led directly to Dan Patch. Savage had reluctantly realized that he couldn't haul his aging horse around forever, so he decided to transport people to the horse. In 1908 he began construction on a short passenger line that connected the Minneapolis streetcar system with a station near his elaborate farm.

Savage incorporated the railroad as the Minneapolis St. Paul Rochester and Dubuque Electric Traction Company, but he promoted it as the "Dan Patch Line" and that name stuck. He advertised heavily, both for investors and riders.

The line did draw people to see the farm and the horses, but not enough. So Savage expanded, adding another attraction ten miles further south. That was Antlers Park, an amusement park and picnicking site on Prairie Lake. He then renamed the lake, not for Dan Patch this time, but for himself. It's still Lake Marion.

The park was successful enough to support the railroad and convince Savage that he should expand the line further, perhaps as far as Iowa. But the Dan Patch Line turned out to be the opposite of the horse it was named for. Instead of being a nearly bottomless source of revenue, it proved to be a money pit on rails. Expansion led to a drain on resources, and by 1914 Savage was having trouble finding new money for expansion. Then, money to pay existing debt became elusive as well. He had actively sold shares in the railroad to small farmers, his long-time customers for feed supplements and Dan Patch White Liniment and Dan Patch Stable Disinfectant. They couldn't be approached a second time.

In 1916, Marion Willis Savage turned fifty-seven and his health was beginning to pay the price for the stress of a failing railroad and a struggling horse breeding operation, both of which had huge operating expenses. In early summer he entered a Minneapolis hospital for a hemorrhoid operation. The procedure was painful and embarrassing but not life threatening.

As Savage recovered from his surgery in the hospital, Dan Patch suddenly fell ill back at the farm. He suffered a mild attack of colic, appeared to recover, and then at 10:00 AM on July 11, Dan Patch collapsed. The men who were with him at his death said that the great horse's legs thrashed in a pacing motion as he died of a massive heart attack.

He was twenty years old, a good old age for a horse who had been so hard used for many of those years, but his death was a shock for the farm workers who were present. Farm manager Murray Anderson wasn't sure how to break the terrible news to Will Savage. Finally he decided to call on the telephone.

Savage appeared to take the news well, although he was surprised and saddened. After all, twenty was about the life expectancy for a horse, no matter how luxurious his surroundings and how much affection was lavished on him. He talked about having Dan Patch mounted so people could still see him.

Less than twenty-four hours after hearing the news about his beloved horse, Marion Willis Savage suffered a pulmonary embolism and died. His family chose not to follow his plans to memorialize Dan Patch, who was buried in an unmarked grave on the farm property. The gravesite has never been found.

Almost every newspaper story of Will Savage's death—and there were hundreds across the country—included Dan Patch's name within the first few sentences. The same was true of the other people connected to Dan, no matter how long they outlived him and what else they did with their lives.

One of them, Myron McHenry, had died in 1911, eight years after leaving the employ of Savage. His life began a downward spiral when he walked away from Dan Patch. At first, he trained a couple of lesser horses for Manley Sturges, then announced he was going to try training Thoroughbreds in New Orleans. But McHenry's greatness was rooted in driving, not training, and his off-and-on training of runners was unsuccessful.

In 1905 his wife Ida divorced him, testifying that he had taken up with a Mrs. Flynn back East. Ida's primary concern was that Myron should have no claim on property she had inherited back home in Illinois. McHenry returned to harness racing full time early in 1911, announcing that he would accept Grand Circuit horses for the season. Friends and admirers on the circuit thought he looked ill but most attributed that to his reputed drinking and advancing age.

In September, at a fair meet in Detroit, McHenry was hospitalized. Three weeks later, his brother Fred and their cousin traveled to Detroit to bring him home to Geneseo, Illinois, where he died on October 29. The local newspaper announced the cause as anemia, but others reported leukemia, which was probably correct. He was not quite fifty-six.

Manley Sturges rated dozens of obituaries upon his death of a stroke in 1921 and every one of them focused on his ownership of Dan Patch, even though he had owned the horse for only one of his seventy-one years. Sturges did accomplish what he had hoped to: he had so thoroughly erased the details of his early life that nobody talked about his long and extremely lucrative career as a gambling operator. Some of his obituaries were actually illustrated with photographs of Frank Knight Sturgis, former president of the New York Stock Exchange, a supporter of Thoroughbred racing and no relation whatsoever to Manley Sturges.

In 1913 Sturges had purchased and enjoyed campaigning a champion pacing mare named Evelyn W. In 1915 he bought the record-holding pacer Directum I from his old friend James Butler. But most of Sturges's post-Dan Patch years were spent trying to become a successful businessman, particularly with a company that planned to build electric rail lines under Manhattan to transport packages. The company failed.

Sturges spent the last couple of years of his life living in an apartment in the Aberdeen Hotel on West 32nd Street, right next door to the site of his Victoria Club. Sturges had a stroke in the spring of 1921 and died a few months later in his nephew's home in Brooklyn. According to papers filed by the nephew, Sturges died without a will and without any real estate or personal property. Apparently he had found a way to hide his money as effectively as he had hidden his other life because at the time of his death, he still owned a desirable four-story building in Manhattan's Washington Mews. The name on the deed was spelled wrong.

His partner Sol Lichtenstein had died in 1918 under mysterious circumstances, killed in a fall from an upper floor of his
apartment building on West End Avenue in New York. By that
time he was well out of the gambling business, although he had
proudly identified himself as a bookmaker in census listings and
city directories throughout the days of the anti-gambling laws
and the near destruction of the racing industry. He did not die
penniless.

Dan Messner remained a well-to-do small town merchant,
dabbling in harness racing and enjoying life as one of the leading
citizens of Oxford, Indiana. He tried for years to live up to his
promise that he would raise another Dan Patch. He eventually owned six full siblings to his great horse, but none ever
amounted to much. Messner died in Oxford in 1936 at the age
of seventy-six, having lived the longest life of anybody associated
with Dan Patch.

Harry Hersey survived them all, dying in Newark, New Jersey,
in 1940 at seventy-three. He was the only one who lived to see
Dan Patch's record of 1:55¼ broken when Billy Direct paced
a mile in 1:55 in Lexington in 1938. Will Savage would have
insisted that Billy Direct only tied Dan's real record, the disallowed mile paced in 1906 at the Minnesota State Fair. Hersey
had left the Stock Farm shortly after Dan's appearance at the
1911 State Fair, at least partially because of Savage's attempts to
make a star out of an unsound Dazzle Patch, Dan's most promising son. He had remained in the racing business with modest
success, finally retiring to New Jersey.

The International 1:55 Stock Farm itself didn't long survive
the deaths of Will Savage and Dan Patch. In 1917 the iconic Taj

Mahal barn burned. In 1918 the Savage heirs sold the land and the new owners later leased it to the operators of a dog track. In 1919 the remaining Savage horses were dispersed. Today there is no evidence of the farm buildings, the training track, and the indoor track that was the talk of racing.

Dan Patch does live on in one sense, however. He's not rated as an outstanding sire, but several of his daughters proved to be excellent broodmares. Two of them figure in the pedigree of a champion of the 1980s named Jate Lobell, who himself turned out to be an outstanding stallion and the sire of hundreds of offspring who would beat Dan Patch's time. Dan's name will survive, probably forever, in the pedigrees of champions.

The International Stock Food Company lasted through the 1930s, and several businesses, particularly tobacco companies, maintained their licenses to use Dan Patch's name and image for decades. The original round of contracts is gone, but there are new cups and plates and model horses featuring Dan Patch.

Most of the racetracks that Dan raced on are gone although the Grand Circuit itself remains. The tracks enjoyed the mixed blessing of possessing large suburban acreage—good for a racing operation but even better for residential development. Glenville, Grosse Pointe, Brighton Beach, Readville, Charter Oak, the Memphis Driving Park—all gone, replaced with houses and other development.

Some of the fairs where Dan Patch appeared continue the tradition of harness racing, as do a handful of fast and important racetracks. The track at Lexington, Kentucky, where Dan Patch made his official record, still operates as the Red Mile and remains one of the fastest in the sport. In Yonkers, the track originally known as Empire City operated for years as Yonkers Raceway. It's enjoyed a rebirth since the addition of a casino. Organizers plucked the name Empire City from the past to adorn their new facility.

As for the sport itself, harness racing has struggled for years. There's too much competition for the betting dollar, and racing's rivals are quicker and easier to play for gamblers. You can scratch a lottery ticket or push a button on a video slot machine in a fraction of the time it takes to read a past performance chart and place a bet.

It's been nearly a century since the average spectator has been able to see an idealized version of himself and his horse in the competitors. Thoroughbred racing has suffered too, although not quite as much since it never relied as harness racing did on the feeling of identity with its audience.

Although diminished, the sport does survive, especially in the Midwest. The addition of casino gambling at many racetracks, despised by people who dream of a return to the glorious days of Star Pointer and Joe Patchen and Dan Patch, has greatly improved the bottom line of the tracks lucky enough to have it. The dreamers are welcome at the surviving racetracks, as are the realists. Harness racing has always welcomed both. In Dan Patch, the sport had a horse that prompted dreams. The reality was right there in the stopwatch.

NOTES ON SOURCES

THERE ARE FOUR previous full-length books that touch on some or most of the aspects of Dan Patch's life, not including the voluminous information published by Marion Willis Savage during his and his horse's lifetimes. The books, all useful in different ways, include Fred Sasse's *The Dan Patch Story,* (The Stackpole Company, 1957) written by a man who met both Dan Patch and Will Savage. *The Dans...And One Was A Pacer,* by Mary Cross, (Oxford, Indiana, 1984), includes interviews of Oxford residents who knew Dan Messner and remembered his horse. Cross also scoured Oxford newspapers for mentions of horse and owner. *The Great Dan and the Remarkable Mr. Savage* by Tim Brady, (Nodin Press, 2006) concentrates especially on the years of Savage's ownership. *Crazy Good,* by Charles Leerhsen, (Simon & Schuster, 2008) is especially good on the competitive racing years. Here are details on other sources:

Prologue

THE STORY OF Walt Disney and Dan Patch is told by several Disney biographers. Especially useful is *The Magic Kingdom: Walt Disney and the American Way of Life*, by Steven Watts (University of Missouri Press, 2002), which gives great detail on Disney's identification with rural and small town America. Leonard Maltin's *The Disney Films* (Hyperion, 1995) details the production process of *So Dear to My Heart.*

Chapter 1

DAN PATCH'S AMERICA

The story of Horatio Alger's rags-to-riches theme is well told in Edwin Palmer Hoyt's *Horatio's Boys: The Life and Works of Horatio Alger, Jr.* (Chilton Book Company, 1974). *Edward Stratemeyer: Creator of the Hardy Boys and Nancy Drew* by Brenda Lange and Kyle Zimmer (Chelsea House, 2003) also mentions his creation of Tom Swift. The movement of the demographic center of population comes from the U.S. Census Bureau. Noel Jacob Kent's *America in 1900* (M.E. Sharpe, Armonk NY 2002) is a fascinating look at the politics and culture in the United States at the turn of the last century as is *1898: The Birth of the American Century,* by David Traxel (Vintage, 1999). *Sport in America: From Wicked Amusement to National Obsession,* edited by David K. Wiggins (Human Kinetics, IL 1994), is an outstanding collection of articles covering American sports history. It is particularly good about early baseball. Details of games and contests come from contemporary newspapers. The Library of Congress' "Chronicling America" section of www.loc.gov includes an excellent selection. Two books provide great detail on harness racing in the nineteenth century. They are Dwight Akers's *Drivers Up: The Story of American Harness Racing* (G. P. Putnam and Sons, 1938) and Philip Pines' *The Complete Book of Harness Racing* (Grosset & Dunlap, 1970). Both are in many libraries and were used in additional chapters as well. *American Media History* by Anthony Fellow (Wadsworth Publishing, 2010) is a highly readable textbook that details the growth of the mass media in the second half of the nineteenth century with much on Pulitzer and inter-newspaper competition.

CHAPTER 2

THE SHOPKEEPER OF OXFORD, INDIANA

Indiana: A Guide to the Hoosier State, published by the Federal Writers' Project in 1941 provides a good overview of the geology, natural resources, and history of the state.

An *Introduction to the Prehistory of Indiana* by James Kellar (Indiana Historical Society, 1974), *The Land of the Miamis* by Elmore Barce (Benton Review, 1922), the *History of Benton County and Historic Oxford,* by Jesse Setlington Burch (Oxford Sesquicentennial Committee, 1928), and the *History of Benton County, Indiana* published by the Benton County Historical Society in 1987 all contributed information, as did Julia Levering's *Historic Indiana* (G. P. Putnam, 1909) which has details about Indiana agriculture and descriptions of country fairs. Most of the details about Dan Messner's background, life in Oxford, and decision to buy a horse come from Mary Cross's *The Dans...And One Was a Pacer,* but other sources include obituaries of all the principal figures published in various newspapers, primarily the Oxford *Tribune.* Much of the information on the history of the Standardbred can be found in *The American Trotter* by John Hervey (Coward-McCann, 1947.)

CHAPTER 3

MR. MESSNER'S BUGGY HORSE

There is no single modern source on the history of pacing genes and the influence of the Narragansett Pacer. One book published not long after the breed disappeared was *Frank Forester's Horse and Horsemanship of the United States and British Provinces of North America* published in 1857 by William H. Herbert (Frank Forester was a pseudonym of William H. Herbert). He includes ten pages on the Narragansett and since people were still living then who actually saw the horses, it is probably the most accurate version available.

CHAPTER 4

MESSNER'S FOLLY

The Care and Training of Trotters and Pacers, published by the *Chicago Horseman* in 1915 gives a good description of breaking, training, and shoeing horses in the era of Dan Patch. The

Government Printing Office's training manual *The Horseshoer*, produced by the U.S. Cavalry in 1926, has been reprinted many times and provides a guide to the prevention of forging and other interference.

Sam Patch was a New England mill worker who, after a downturn in the textile business, figured out that he might make money if he could only find himself a little celebrity. In 1927 he leaped across the Passaic Falls in New Jersey, earning newspaper headlines and some cash. In 1828 Patch jumped into the Hudson River from the mast of a sloop, a leap of ninety feet, to the delight of five hundred spectators. He followed the next year with leaps over a section of Niagara Falls and one over the Genesee Falls in upstate New York. He failed to come up from the water on that final jump.

He was already known as the "Brave Patch" and the "Wonderful Patch" and the "Great Patch" and these names survived him. The names, which equally applied to the horse, may have been the origin of the story that Dan was named for Sam. "The Wonderful Leaps of Sam Patch" by Richard Dorson in the December 1966 edition of *American Heritage* sums up his story, but there is also a recent biography, *Sam Patch, the Famous Jumper* (Hill and Wang, 2003).

CHAPTER 5

A RACEHORSE AFTER ALL
The evolution of the sulky is well covered in the Akers and Pines book and is discussed in detail in "Perfecting the Sulky" by Bruce

Stearns in the March 1983 issue of *Hoofbeats*. The Harness Racing Museum and Hall of Fame has a fascinating display of historic sulkies as well as information on the change from high wooden wheels to the low wire and rubber bicycle wheels. The museum is in Goshen, New York, in the region where Hambletonian spent his stud career.

CHAPTER 6

ON THE WINGS OF THE WIND
The story of the McHenry family comes from genealogical data and land records of Kentucky and Illinois. The family background of William McHenry, a state senator who served in the Illinois legislature with Abraham Lincoln, is mentioned in many early Illinois histories, biographical collections, as well as histories of White County, where the McHenrys originally settled, and McHenry County, named for him. William was the great uncle of Myron. McHenry descendant Donna Buechler of Geneseo, Illinois, where Myron McHenry grew up, provided other family stories and details of his death.

CHAPTER 7

A STAR IS BORN
The story of the Glenville track is told in *Sports in Cleveland: An Illustrated History* by John Grabowski (Indiana University Press, 1992) and the *Encyclopedia of Cleveland History* edited

by Grabowski and David Dirck Van Tassel (Indiana University Press, 1997). One version of the invention of pacing hopples as told by John Hervey was reprinted in *Hoofbeats* in May 1968, but another more contemporary version was told in wire service articles about the death of John Browning, the presumed inventor, in June, 1905. Among the newspapers was the Otago, New Zealand, *Witness,* June 28, 1905. The fact that auto races were held at Grosse Pointe and other tracks on the early Grand Circuit has helped to keep their histories alive, even though most of the tracks and horses are long gone. British researcher Darren Galpin has assembled a useful list of tracks used for auto competition before World War I, including many which hosted the Grand Circuit. His list, which is available at several places online, includes detailed descriptions of the tracks.

CHAPTER 8

THE BIG STAGE

Dwight Akers *Drivers Up,* previously mentioned, has several sections on early harness racing in New York, as well as the state of racing in the metropolitan area at the turn of the last century. "A Roadway Built for the Elite to Trot Out Their Rigs" by Christopher Gray in the *New York Times,* July 13, 1997, gave additional details about the Harlem River Speedway, and the professional gambling situation is thoroughly discusses in Steven A. Riess's *The Sport of Kings and the Kings of Crime: Horse Racing, Politics, and Organized Crime in New York 1965-1913* (Syracuse University Press, 2011) although he says little about harness racing.

CHAPTER 9

A GAMBLER TAKES A CHANCE

The story of Manley Sturges was pieced together from different mostly unrelated sources, a necessary approach because of the way he compartmentalized his life. Information on his family background and early life can be found in standard genealogical sources, including Federal and New York Census reports from 1850 through 1920. The historian for Wayne County, NY, has a file, including a photograph somewhat different from the one printed in the *Horse Review* at the time of his death. There is no source for this photograph, so I have used the printed one, assuming that the racing newspaper editor knew what Dan Patch's owner looked like. Some family history comes from biographies of Manley's cousin Charles Sturges, the one-time mayor of Saratoga Springs, NY. One is *Our County and Its People: A Descriptive and Biographical Record of Saratoga County, New York*, published by the *Saratogian* newspaper in 1899. Also useful on the story of Sturges's hometown and background is *History, Reminiscences, Anecdotes and Legends of Great Sodus Bay, Sodus Point, Sloop Landing, Sodus Village, Pultneyville, Maxwell* by Walter Henry Green (Sodus, NY, 1947). Sturges's time at the Bayshore House and his relationship to George Emery and the Pavilion is told in snippets in local newspapers including the *Wayne County Alliance*, the *Wayne County Review*, the Sodus *Record*, the *Lake Shore News* of Wolcott, NY, and the *Arcadian Weekly Gazette* of Newark, NY. All considered him a local and reported his comings and goings throughout his life without reference to his gambling career. The Syracuse *Post-Standard* covered the Sodus area as part of its region and many pre-1895 articles provide clues to his activities at Sodus Bay. His Manhattan history is assembled from census, real estate, and city directories from 1892 through the end of his life, plus brief references in all the New York City newspapers, including the *Times,* the *World,* the *Herald,* and the Brooklyn *Eagle.*

CHAPTER 10

RACE AGAINST TIME

The early history of Marion Willis comes from standard genealogical sources, as well as *Herbert Hoover's Hometown: The Story of West Branch* by Maud Stratton (West Branch, Iowa, 1948). Also important to Savage's early interest in horse racing was the *History of Muscatine County Iowa* (Western Historical Company, 1879) which includes a section on the importation of the Bashaw horses. Savage himself talks about the Bashaws and his own Golden Bashaw in the *International Stock Food Company Yearbook (*Minneapolis, 1905). The best work on Savage's early years in the patent medicine business is Brady's *The Great Dan Patch and the Remarkable Mr. Savage,* mentioned earlier. *The Toadstool Millionaires: A Social History of Patent Medicines in America Before Federal Regulation* by James Harvey Young (Princeton University Press, 1972) provides good background on the subject, although Savage is not mentioned. Two booklets that have information on both the pre-Dan Patch and later years were compiled by Willis Ackerman: *Dan Patch: Mass Merchandiser* (Osseo, MN, 1981) and *Dan Patch: M.W. Savage Update* (Osseo, MN, 1984).

CHAPTER 11

FAME AND FORTUNE

Information about the actual time trials and other public events are reported in dozens of newspapers throughout the entire time of Dan Patch's racing career. In addition, Savage himself gave great detail of the events in his *International Stock Food Farm Yearbook,* mentioned previously, especially those in 1903 and 1904. He included his own observations on the demonstrations and reprinted the most favorable newspaper articles.

CHAPTER 12

FINISH LINE

Dan Patch and other International Stock Food advertisements featuring him can be found in most newspapers printed in the Midwest and in agriculture- and horse-related magazines between January of 1903 and early 1916. The largest number appeared from 1908 to 1911, after newspaper coverage of Dan Patch had waned. The Aberdeen Hotel, where Manley Sturges lived after leaving the Victoria Club, still exists and still operates as a hotel. It's now the La Quinta Manhattan, in the middle of "Koreatown" on W. Thirty-Second Street. The Victoria building itself is gone. The story of Dan Patch's descendants appeared in "Reviving the Legacy of Dan Patch" by Dean Hoffman in *Hoofbeats,* February, 1987.

APPENDIX

WAS MANLEY STURGES THE REAL GATSBY?

MANLEY STURGES WAS directly involved with Dan Patch for less than ten months. He completed his purchase in mid-March 1902, sold the horse in early December, and walked away from the story. In addition to fame, which he didn't particularly want, and profit, which must have been appreciated, his brief ownership of Dan Patch gave Sturges something he did greatly desire: the completion of his transformation.

It was actually his second reinvention. He had been born into a respectable but hardly affluent family in a tiny town on the shores of Lake Ontario and had made himself into a wealthy Manhattanite, thanks to success in criminal business activities. But he effectively hid the source of his income and, after his Dan

Patch year, Manley Sturges found himself reborn as a respectable businessman.

It's almost as if Jay Gatsby, having made himself rich in bootlegging and bond theft, gave up illegal booze distribution and became the pharmacy owner he claimed to be, thanks to his brief affair with Daisy Buchanan. Gatsby, in F. Scott Fitzgerald's great novel, managed only the first half of his transformation. He had been a poor young man from South Dakota, discovered on the shores of Lake Superior, and reinvented as a rich Manhattanite, thanks to his success in criminal activities.

Gatsby was murdered by the husband of Daisy's hit-and-run victim and never got the chance for the second half of the transformation. But the comparisons with Manley Sturges are obvious and there is the intriguing possibility that Dan Patch's second owner was more than simply Gatsby-like.

To be sure, Sturges was a generation older than Scott Fitzgerald. He died in 1921, at least two years before Fitzgerald began work on *The Great Gatsby*. But there are tantalizing traces of Manley Sturges in Jay Gatsby, both in his back story and in the arc of his transformation.

Ever since the novel was published in 1925, the identity of the "real Gatsby" has been a subject of gossip and guesses. Gatsby was undoubtedly a composite character, at least partly autobiographical. Several names other than Fitzgerald have emerged as possibilities for the original Gatsby, some more likely than others. Manley Sturges has never been mentioned, probably because of the time frame and the nature of the criminal activities, but he's a more likely candidate than some accepted contenders.

Conventional wisdom in the Gatsby guessing game has it that the bootlegger model was a man named Max Gerlach, who apparently did distribute illegal liquor during Prohibition and may have known Fitzgerald. The alcoholic author was a big consumer while he was writing his most famous novel. Gerlach, a native New Yorker, had a background that was nothing like Gatsby's, but he is said to have used Gatsby's favorite phrase, "old sport." Zelda Fitzgerald, late in her life, referred in a letter to a man named Gerlach as a model for Gatsby.

Among Gatsby's crimes was the apparent sale of stolen bonds and perhaps stock fraud. Many observers look to Edward M. Fuller as a Gatsby model. Fuller lived in Great Neck on Long Island, reborn as Fitzgerald's West Egg, prior to the time the Fitzgeralds lived there. They were in Great Neck in 1923 and 1924, when Scott Fitzgerald conceived and may have begun writing *The Great Gatsby.*

Fuller was charged in a celebrated stock fraud and Fitzgerald himself referred to reading up on the Fuller case as he was sharpening the character of Gatsby. It doesn't appear that Fitzgerald ever met Fuller, but the case was in the news during his Great Neck months. Fuller seems a likely model for Gatsby's bond fraud escapade, but his background was nothing like Gatsby's either. He had a law degree, had been a stockbroker in Chicago early in the century, and had worked out of the same brokerage office in Manhattan since 1903. Edward M. Fuller was no mystery man, although he was a white collar criminal, and he was not self-invented.

The wide-open Long Island house parties given by Gatsby mirrored those thrown by Herbert Bayard Swope, a newspaper editor whose summer home was near the Fitzgerald house in Great Neck. The Fitzgeralds attended regularly until their drunken escapades had them banished by Swope's wife. Nothing else about Swope suggests Gatsby although he, like Fuller, was friendly with the notorious gangster Arnold Rothstein.

Rothstein, whom Fitzgerald claimed to have met once, also figures in *The Great Gatsby*. Most literary scholars believe Rothstein was the model for Meyer Wolfsheim, Gatsby's mentor, employer, and business partner. Wofsheim is described by Gatsby as "the man who fixed the World Series back in 1919" which Arnold Rothstein was widely (but probably inaccurately) believed to have done in real life. But Rothstein was urbane and well dressed, while Fitzgerald presents Wolfsheim as a caricature of a Jewish New Yorker. He suggests that Gatsby was a gentlemanly-appearing Gentile front for Wolfsheim.

"I understand you're looking for a business gonnegtion," Wolfsheim says to narrator Nick Carraway after being introduced by Gatsby. So, a few people think, the well-spoken Rothstein must have been a model for Gatsby instead. But if you leave out the 1919 World Series incident as a device to bring the story into the 1920s and look further back for a heavily accented underworld figure, you reach Sol Lichtenstein, bookmaker and casino owner. His partner was the gentlemanly-appearing Gentile Manley Sturges.

We don't know what Lichtenstein sounded like, but one author who heard him speak quotes him as saying "Ve vas attagged in the rear!" in describing an incident in Delmonico's restaurant when a group of regular patrons tried to dislodge a table of bookmakers. The story was meant to be comical,

So Lichtenstein, the leading oddsmaker at New York racetracks and partner of Manley Sturges is shown in a 1905 newspaper cartoon.

but it does show that Lichtenstein was known to be heavily accented.

Neither Sturges nor Lichtenstein was involved in bootlegging, since the sale of liquor was not illegal while they were running their gambling clubs. But gambling certainly was and they, like Gatsby and Wolfsheim, made hundreds of thousands of dollars while staying a step ahead of the law.

Sturges's early life is much closer to Gatsby's than those of Gerlach, Fuller, or Rothstein. He was not a midwesterner like Gatsby, but he was from far upstate New York and grew up on the shores of one of the Great Lakes. Sturges's Lake Ontario is

The Empire City racetrack, built by William H. Clark and owned by
Sturges's business partner James Butler, is shown in a 1905 postcard.

actually closer to Fitzgerald's description than is Gatsby's Lake
Superior. Gatsby fishes for salmon in Superior, which has no
salmon, while Ontario in the nineteenth century had a species
of trout known as lake salmon.

Other similarities: a treacherous sandbar plays a major part
in Fitzgerald's book, while Sturges's Sodus Bay features a nearly
mile and a half sandbar now known as Crescent Beach. Gatsby
was discovered and taken out of Little Girl Bay by an uncouth
Montana copper baron named Dan Cody, whom Gatsby had
rescued from a sandbar. As far as we can tell, Sturges took
himself out of Sodus Bay, although he probably met someone
who encouraged him to go to New York. But Sturges did have a
connection with an uncouth Montana copper baron, or at least
everybody thought he did.

The magnificent Empire City Trotting Park, purchased in turn by Sturges's employer or partner Frank Farrell and Sturges's business partner James Butler was built by William H. Clark, who was sometimes identified at the time and is still often described as "copper magnate William H. Clark." William H. Clark was a Tammany Hall lawyer. William A. Clark was the sometimes-uncouth Montana copper baron.

Although he liked racing and sometimes drove on the Speedway, William A. did not build Empire City. The mistake still goes on in publicity materials for what's now Yonkers Raceway at Empire City. The wrong William Clark was often given credit for the racetrack throughout the twentieth century and Fitzgerald may well have heard the mistaken story.

There are clues in Fitzgerald's letters that somebody other than Max Gerlach or Edward M. Fuller contributed to the concept of Gatsby. Responding to editor Max Perkins's complaints that the first draft of Gatsby was a little vague, Fitzgerald admitted that he originally had no idea what Gatsby looked like or what criminal activity he was actually engaged in. He had his wife Zelda draw portraits until he felt he knew his title character.

If Fitzgerald knew Max Gerlach the bootlegger well enough to make him a model, he knew what Gerlach looked like and what he did. In Edward Fuller's case, the story of the trial, complete with photographs, stared out from every newspaper. Fitzgerald should have known what Fuller looked like as well.

But Manley Sturges would have been faceless to Fitzgerald. He was rarely photographed, and if the two men met (and there is a faint possibility that they did) Sturges would have been a much older man at that time than he had been at the height of his criminal career.

Any possibility that Manley Sturges made up part of Jay Gatsby depends on whether Scott Fitzgerald could have heard anything about Sturges's criminal career. And if Fitzgerald did, would he have paid attention? The answer is yes to both parts of the question.

Fitzgerald couldn't have avoided hearing about Dan Patch during his childhood years in St. Paul, Minnesota, although he was never a particular fan of racing. He was born there in 1896 but left with his parents as a young child. He came back often to visit relatives and the family returned for good in 1908.

Dan Patch, following his Sturges year, lived in Hamilton, Minnesota (renamed Savage), about fifteen miles south of St. Paul. During his thirteen years there, from 1903 to 1916, he was one of the leading residents of the Twin Cities, the subject of countless newspaper stories, the star of dozens of local public appearances, and the hero of several parades in Minneapolis and St. Paul. Scott Fitzgerald knew all about Dan Patch.

He never wrote about seeing the horse, but he made a journal notation of his visit to the Minnesota State Fair on its opening day in 1911. The most publicized attraction that day was an appearance by Dan Patch.

The name stayed with him. The hero of Fitzgerald's second novel, *The Beautiful and Damned*, was named Anthony Patch. It's likely that anybody offering Scott Fitzgerald information about a former owner of Dan Patch, perhaps after learning that the young author was from St. Paul, would have found an eager audience.

James Butler, grocery tycoon, horse owner, and racetrack operator, was a friend and business associate of Manley Sturges. (Photo: *Munsey's Magazine* December 1904)

Who would that have been? Probably one of two men, or possibly both. Fitzgerald arrived at Princeton University in September 1913 where he almost immediately became involved with the Triangle Club, an organization that produced an annual original musical. Fitzgerald took part in at least three productions during his college career and hoped to become club president. Among the club's distinguished patrons during the years Fitzgerald was at Princeton were Mr. and Mrs. Adrian H. Larkin. Their nephew John Adrian Larkin was the immediate outgoing president of the Triangle Club when Fitzgerald arrived. Fitzgerald probably met all the Larkins, who attended most performances in the New York area, some time in 1914 or 1915.

Larkin was a Wall Street lawyer, a well-established member of New York society, and a business partner during that same period of Manley E. Sturges in Electric Carrier, a company that was developing a subway mail carrier system. It's not known if Sturges and Larkin were social friends as well as partners, but Larkin

Herbert Bayard Swope, newspaper reporter and editor, told stories of New York gambling to F. Scott Fitzgerald. *(Photo: Library of Congress)*

had represented Sturges's friend and business associate James Butler during Butler's purchase of the Empire City racetrack a dozen years earlier.

It's also not known if Sturges attended any Triangle performances with his partner Larkin, although he may have. It does seem unlikely that either man would have told a young undergraduate any details about an illicit career, but they could have been interested in the fact that Fitzgerald was from the Twin Cities and told him about Sturges's relationship to Dan Patch.

The more likely source of information about Manley Sturges's earlier career was a man who has already figured in the Gatsby story. Herbert Bayard Swope, who gave the Gatsby-style house parties, was equally a lover of horse racing and of casino-style gambling. His preference was Thoroughbred racing, but he would bet on horses of any breed.

Swope first arrived in Manhattan, from St. Louis by way of Chicago, early in 1902 to begin work as a reporter on the New York *Herald*. He immediately began a lifetime of exploring the city's gambling venues and became a friend or acquaintance

Davey Johnson, one of the most successful gambling entrepreneurs, bought the Victoria Club from Sturges and Lichtenstein and was a friend of Herbert Bayard Swope. (Photo: Library of Congress)

of every significant player in the gambling scene, probably including Manley Sturges.

Swope reached New York just as Sturges was looking to ease out of the illegal casino business but in plenty of time to hear about and probably report on how one of his new acquaintances was buying and then campaigning a celebrated horse. It's impossible to know most of the subjects Swope covered for the *Herald* since bylines were rarely given then, but he most likely wrote at least some of the newspaper's articles about Dan Patch.

Sturges and Swope may have known each other personally, since Swope probably would have made it his business to meet him, but at the very least they had friends in common. Swope became well known as a friendly acquaintance of Davey Johnson, who bought the Victoria Club from Sturges and Lichtenstein and may have been their partner for a year or two. Swope would have known as much of the truth about Manley Sturges as anybody did.

The New York *World,* which Swope joined in 1909 as a reporter, gave him his entrée into society. He became rich and renowned as a crusading reporter and later as an editor. By

1920 he had eased back on his friendships with gamblers and underworld figures, replacing them in his circle of his friends with people in the arts. When Scott and Zelda Fitzgerald arrived in Great Neck in the fall of 1922, they joined Swope's circle.

Fitzgerald had already become famous as the author of the *This Side of Paradise,* a groundbreaking novel of the younger generation, and Swope was happy to include the celebrated young author in the audience for his tales of the older generation in New York. There were many story-telling sessions during the summer of 1923, just as Scott Fitzgerald was developing his concept for *The Great Gatsby.*

The evidence for Manley Sturges as a model for Jay Gatsby is entirely circumstantial. But the circumstances exist. Sturges was much like Gatsby in his background, his ambition to be accepted in honest society, and his willingness to work outside the law to earn the money to help with the acceptance. Fitzgerald had the opportunity to hear about Sturges and likely the interest, given that he and Dan Patch hailed from the same area. At this point, nearly a hundred years later, the connection can't be proved, but it can't be disproved either. Sturges deserves to be considered seriously as a contributor to the Gatsby character.

Appendix Notes

Almost all biographies of F. Scott Fitzgerald discuss his development of the Jay Gatsby character. More detailed is *F. Scott Fitzgerald's The Great Gatsby,* part of literary critic Harold Bloom's *Bloom's Guides* series (Chelsea House, 2006). The best discussion of potential real-life Gatsbys is found in scholar Matthew Bruccoli's *F. Scott Fitzgerald's The Great Gatsby: A Documentary Volume* (Gale Group, 2007). Bruccoli, who was particularly fond of the Gerlach comparison, was a prolific writer on the Gatsby character. More information on the correspondence related to the character's development is in *Max Perkins: Editor of Genius* by A. Scott Berg (E. P. Dutton, 1978). *Man of the World* by Alfred Allan Lewis (Bobbs-Merrill, 1978) tells the story of Herbert Bayard Swope and his relationship to gambling, gamblers, and Fitzgerald. *Inventing Great Neck: Jewish Identity and the American Dream,* by Judith S. Goldstein (Rutgers University Press, 2006) has details of the Swope parties. The information about Adrian Larkin comes from newspaper articles, primarily in the *New York Times,* about the Empire City racetrack, Princeton Triangle Club performances, and the business dealings of the Carrier Electric Company, owned by Sturges and Larkin. Stories about Sol Lichtenstein are in *Delmonico's: A Century of Splendor* by Lately Thomas (Houghton-Mifflin, 1967) as well as newspaper stories of the era.

INDEX